RESULTS BASED FACILITATION

MOVING FROM TALK » TO ACTION

2ND EDITION

FOUNDATION SKILLS

BOOK 1

IN MEETINGS

IN NEIGHBORHOODS
AND ORGANIZATIONS

IN COMMUNITIES

BY JOLIE BAIN PILLSBURY, Ph.D.   A PUBLICATION OF SHERBROOKE CONSULTING, INC.   ARLINGTON, VA

Results Based Facilitation: Book One – Foundation Skills – 2nd Edition
ISBN: 9780989017732 (Print Version)

ISBN: 9780989017763 (Kindle)

Sherbrooke Consulting, Inc.
1500 22nd Street North
Arlington, VA 22209
www. sherbrookeconsulting.com
www.rbl-apps.com

Early in my career, I learned to facilitate as a necessity. As a member of an executive team in a large public agency, my role was to support frontline workers in a series of successive transformations to improve results for the people we served. Through that work, I discovered the hard way that I could not accomplish my goals without developing and using facilitation skills. Those same facilitation skills proved invaluable in numerous roles — facilitator, consultant, team leader, coach, and meeting participant. Results Based Facilitation (RBF) is the distillation of what I learned about what it takes for groups to make, own, and implement decisions.

If learning to facilitate was a necessity, helping others learn to facilitate was a choice. In the past two decades, I have facilitated large and small meetings in all 50 states and worked as a facilitator with thousands of people. Often after a meeting, people come up to me and say, "I think we need to be able to have these kinds of meetings even when you are not with us" or "How did you learn to facilitate?"

These questions led to my developing workshops and materials to build the facilitation skills of others. Making the methods accessible and transferable was as hard, challenging, and exciting as was developing the approach. And this process, as is often the case, made both the method and the instruction more *effective* — especially since at every step of the way the learning, discovery, and development process was itself a team effort.

At its heart, RBF is an integrated set of competencies that provide the skills people need to make a measurable difference. RBF meetings result in action plans that, when implemented, accelerate the pace of positive change.

The most difficult and most powerful RBF practice is the ability to focus on, have conversations about, and work toward a common result. In programs where people were supported by and learned RBF skills, those most highly valued were those that helped ensure decision making to achieve common results.[1] Similarly, research on the effects of RBF skill development undertaken by five California county health teams demonstrated that people could not only hold results-focused conversations, but that they valued the success of their efforts.[2]

EVEN THOUGH THE CONVERSATION
TO AGREE ON THE TARGET RESULT
WAS HARD, WE WERE ABLE TO DO IT.

AFTERWARDS I HEARD FROM ONE
OF THE OTHER LEADERS THAT THIS
WAS THE BEST, MOST FOCUSED
MEETING HE HAD EVER BEEN TO ...
WE AGREED ON THE RESULT AND
THEN MOVED TO ACTION.

- CALIFORNIA COUNTY HEALTH OFFICIAL'S
FEEDBACK ON USING RBF COMPETENCIES

"As you can see from the flow chart, the problem stems from a lack of direction."

DO THE DIFFICULT THINGS WHILE THEY ARE EASY AND DO THE GREAT THINGS WHILE THEY ARE SMALL. A JOURNEY OF A THOUSAND MILES MUST BEGIN WITH A SINGLE STEP.

- LAO TZU

This evidence of effective methods is significant because meetings are problematic. Whether it's a one-on-one phone conversation, folks chatting around the water cooler, or a huge gathering from different departments, viewpoints, even cultures, meetings fuel collective action and collective impact. They're the lubricant that keeps people advancing — except that too often, far from smoothing the way, they actually stall movement. Moving to action ought to be simple. After all, people deal with one another through talk, words, language, and expression. Conversation is the way we articulate the results we seek for our organization and plan how to get them.

But simply articulating ways to solve problems doesn't produce results. All too often, meetings become occasions for cross talk, for wasting time, for generating feelings of frustration and even anger, for failing to seize opportunities, and for giving up. The challenge is to move meetings from talk to the actions that get results, to break the deadlock, to get organizations unstuck from the meeting paralysis that can leave people feeling so helpless and exhausted.

The solution, practical for both facilitators and participants, consists of learning and practicing skills that create the shift from talk to action. Using these skills achieves not only the set of results sought but also meaningful conversations and relationships that add value and bring satisfaction to those involved.

Learning the skills needed provides the *how* of doing better. Competency in these skills translates theory into practice and makes it possible for people with disparate interests, values, cultures, and authority structures to move off square one, align their actions, and achieve commonly sought results that can be measured.

RBF defines and describes each needed skill and provides exercises for competency in each, from basic through advanced skills.

Self-assessment tools are included for each skill so people can track their progress and pinpoint areas where they need more practice. A distinguishing feature of learning these skills is that people are asked to use each skill immediately, integrating practice of the skill into daily activities so as to build mastery — and see results — day after day.

The good news is that anybody can use RBF skills at any time to hold more productive meetings:

> Line managers, frontline supervisors, and senior leaders who want a practical approach that works in their complex realities.

> Teachers, coaches, and facilitators who want to take their skills and abilities to the next level and obtain better results with their students and clients.

> Board members who want to hold their organizations accountable.

- » Doctors and nurses who want to improve the quality of care for their patients.

- » Community leaders who want to collaborate to get things done.

- » Nonprofit leaders and managers who want to show results to their funders, and funders who want to have a tangible, measurable, meaningful return on their investment.

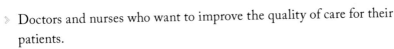

Over the years, people in all these roles have used RBF skills to accomplish their goals. However, each faced the same challenge — how to act on what they knew or integrate a new behavior or way of thinking into what they practiced on a daily basis. This is the gap between people knowing and doing. How do adults with established attitudes and behaviors move to new attitudes and behaviors — especially when those adults come from different backgrounds with different values, cultures, and interests?

Based on research and practice, RBF offers a solution that people can apply in their daily work. RBF has proven time and again to produce conversations and meetings that prompt direct action. Thanks to the experimentation, application, and discipline of the many RBF thought and practice partners, *Results Based Facilitation: Book One — Foundation Skills* can help you in three ways to hold more productive meetings.

1. RBF is a specific, hands-on method that enables people both to understand what they need to do and why they need to do it, and to practice on a daily basis the skills for getting different and better results in their meetings and conversations. While most books on leadership exhort people to be better listeners, rarely, however, do you see leaders and managers who actually practice listening well. *Results Based Facilitation: Book One — Foundation Skills* goes beyond exhortation to provide the specific preparation steps, practice steps, and relapse strategies to achieve better listening.

2. RBF is designed to empower people to get concrete, actionable results anywhere, any time. The method is useful in one-on-one conversations, small groups, and large groups whether you are a meeting participant, meeting convener, or meeting facilitator.

3. RBF complements and strengthens any other method a leader, manager, consultant, facilitator, or supervisor already uses. It specifically helps people map what they already know and do, empowering them to use existing competencies to do better — for better results more consistently and more frequently.

The following thought partners and practitioners have helped advance the work of RBF through their willingness to practice and use the skills. It is with great appreciation that I acknowledge their efforts to improve the well-being of children, families, and communities:

THERE HAS RARELY IN MY WORK LIFE BEEN A COURSE OR WORKSHOP THAT HAS IMPACTED MY DAY-TO-DAY WORK AS MUCH AS THE RESULTS BASED FACILITATION TRAINING. THERE IS SOMETHING VERY POWERFUL AND TRANSFORMATIVE ABOUT ATTENDING A TRAINING WITH THE PEOPLE YOU WORK WITH AND THEN HAVING THE ORGANIZATION EMBRACE IT.

- PARTICIPANT, 2013 RESULTS BASED FACILITATION WORKSHOP

>> *Victoria Goddard-Truitt,* cofounder of the RBF Network and the Results Based Leadership Consortium, editor of *Introduction to Results Based Facilitation: An RBF Primer* and *Theory of Aligned Contributions* and thought partner in development of the practice methods.

>> *Raj Chawla,* cofounder of the Results Based Leadership Consortium, coauthor of many of the results based leadership applications, and dedicated practice and thought partner in using and coaching RBF skills.

>> *Steven Jones,* cofounder of the RBF Network, and *Phyllis Rozansky,* for their continued commitment to building the RBF skills of leaders to achieve results.

>> *Ron Redmon, Kathleen Pogue White,* and *Mark Friedman,* whose work has informed the development of the RBF skills.

>> *Annetta Berry, Sayge Medlin, John Bringuel,* and *the hundreds of Georgia Policy Connection RBF Practitioners,* for their dedication to learning and using RBF skills in service to the children and families of their state.

>> *Alice Shobe,* for her leadership in leveraging RBF in efforts to end homelessness in Washington state.

>> *The New Haven and Connecticut Results Coaches and Elm City Fellows,* for using RBF skills to improve conditions of well-being in their communities.

>> *The leaders in Marion County/Indianapolis and Elkhart County, Indiana,* for applying RBF to achieve successful ex-offender reentry in their communities.

>> *The leaders in Baltimore City, Anne Arundel County, Maryland, and DeKalb County, Georgia,* for their application of RBF to help children enter school ready to learn.

>> *The leaders in the Arlington Public School District,* for their application of RBF to address disparities in educational outcomes.

>> *Steve Schroeder, Connie Revell, Catherine Saucedo, Reason Reyes,* and *the staff of the University of California Smoking Cessation Leadership Center,* for their application of RBF to improve health and help people quit smoking.

>> *Donna Stark, Barbara Squires, Jennifer Gross,* and *Ashley Stewart,* thought partners and practitioners at the Annie E. Casey Foundation, who use RBF in their work to improve the well-being of the country's most vulnerable families.

>> *Kate Shatzkin, Shagas Design, Victoria Goddard-Truitt,* and other members of the editing and design team who worked so hard to produce *RBF Foundation Skills, second edition.*

My deepest gratitude goes to Robert D. Pillsbury, my husband and cofounder of the Results Based Facilitation Network. This work would not have been possible without his helpful insights, unflagging support, extraordinary creativity as an iconographer, and lifelong commitment to be being my closest thought and practice partner.

Jolie Bain Pillsbury, Ph.D. (ENTJ)
President, Sherbrooke Consulting, Inc.
Cofounder, RBF Network
Cofounder, Results Based Leadership Consortium
December 2015

NOTES:

[1] Littlefield, O'Brien, and Hersey. *Participant or Spectator: Non-profit Engagement in Multi-Sector Collaboratives.* American Society for Public Administration Conference. Baltimore, MD. March 2011.

[2] Pillsbury and Pillsbury. *A Teachable Method for Changing Unhealthy Behavior.* SBIR Grant 1R43DA022070-01A1. April 2008.

IMPORTANT ICONS

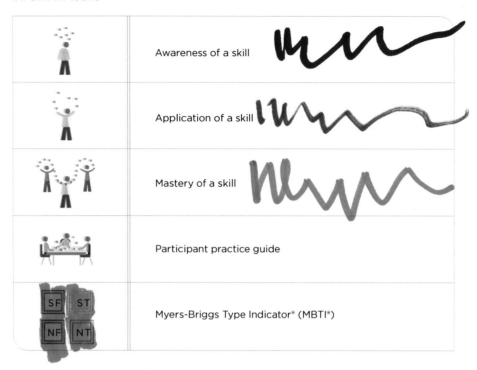

	Awareness of a skill
	Application of a skill
	Mastery of a skill
	Participant practice guide
	Myers-Briggs Type Indicator® (MBTI®)

GLOSSARY OF ACRONYMS

ACRONYM	FULL NAME OR PHRASE
3Rs	Results, Relationships, and Resources
ARE	Acknowledge, Rephrase, and Explore
B/ART	Boundaries of Authority, Role, and Task
CS	Context Statement
EQ	Effective Question
LF	Listen For
MBTI®	Myers-Briggs Type Indicator®
PBDM	Proposal-Based Decision Making
PRS	Person-Role-System
RBF	Results Based Facilitation
RBL	Results-Based Leadership
SBI	Situation, Behavior, Impact

The second editions of the two books *Results Based Facilitation: Book One — Foundation Skills* and *Results Based Facilitation: Book Two — Advanced Skills* present proven practice methods and competencies that help people work together to make meaningful and visible improvement in the lives of children, adults, and families. Over the past 15 years, thousands of leaders and facilitators have used Results Based Facilitation (RBF) in service to their organizations, neighborhoods, and communities. From their application of the methods and competencies, evidence is emerging that practicing RBF leads to productive meetings that move people to results.

WHAT IS RESULTS BASED FACILITATION?

Results Based Facilitation is a competency-based approach to participating in and facilitating meetings that get results. The six RBF competencies move groups from talk to action by focusing on meeting results and by developing an accountability framework for commitments to aligned action. RBF produces results within programs, as well as for organizations and communities. RBF skills ensure that participants, conveners, and facilitators work together, entering a meeting with results in mind and leaving with action commitments in hand.

WHAT ARE RESULTS BASED FACILITATION COMPETENCIES AND SKILLS?

RBF consists of six competencies that enable groups to act collaboratively, make decisions together, identify how as individuals and as a group they can contribute to accelerating action to achieve observable results, and commit to take those actions in an aligned way after the meeting.

The six RBF competencies are the following:

1. Hold Roles
2. Hold Conversations
3. Hold Groups
4. Hold 3R Meetings
5. Hold Mental Models
6. Hold Action and Results

ENTER WITH RESULTS IN MIND
AND LEAVE WITH ACTION
COMMITMENTS IN HAND

The last two competencies are the subject of the next book, *Results Based Facilitation: Book Two — Advanced Skills* (abbreviated as Book Two). The six competencies, a brief description, and the associated 22 distinct skills are listed in the table below.

THE SIX RBF COMPETENCIES AND 22 SKILLS

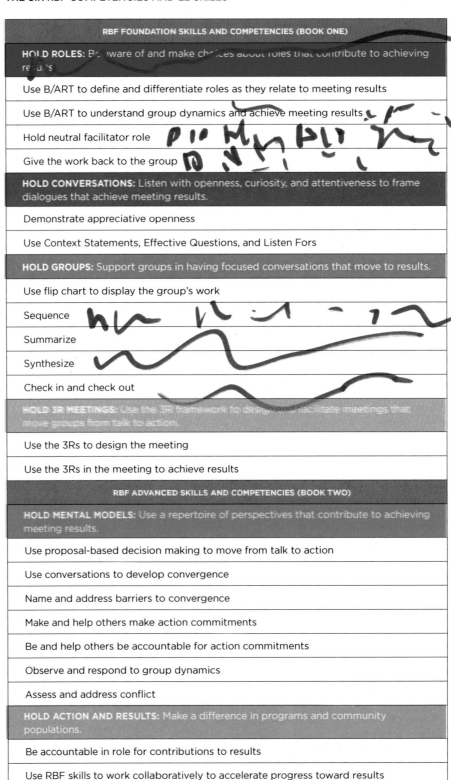

RBF FOUNDATION SKILLS AND COMPETENCIES (BOOK ONE)
HOLD ROLES: Be aware of and make choices about roles that contribute to achieving results.
Use B/ART to define and differentiate roles as they relate to meeting results
Use B/ART to understand group dynamics and achieve meeting results
Hold neutral facilitator role
Give the work back to the group
HOLD CONVERSATIONS: Listen with openness, curiosity, and attentiveness to frame dialogues that achieve meeting results.
Demonstrate appreciative openness
Use Context Statements, Effective Questions, and Listen Fors
HOLD GROUPS: Support groups in having focused conversations that move to results.
Use flip chart to display the group's work
Sequence
Summarize
Synthesize
Check in and check out
HOLD 3R MEETINGS: Use the 3R framework to design and facilitate meetings that move groups from talk to action.
Use the 3Rs to design the meeting
Use the 3Rs in the meeting to achieve results
RBF ADVANCED SKILLS AND COMPETENCIES (BOOK TWO)
HOLD MENTAL MODELS: Use a repertoire of perspectives that contribute to achieving meeting results.
Use proposal-based decision making to move from talk to action
Use conversations to develop convergence
Name and address barriers to convergence
Make and help others make action commitments
Be and help others be accountable for action commitments
Observe and respond to group dynamics
Assess and address conflict
HOLD ACTION AND RESULTS: Make a difference in programs and community populations.
Be accountable in role for contributions to results
Use RBF skills to work collaboratively to accelerate progress toward results

Each of the 22 skills is described in terms of three levels of mastery — developing awareness of the skill, applying the skill, and mastering the skill. A series of questions are provided to help readers self-assess their current skill level. Skill levels are not discrete but rather steps along a continuum, represented by arrows leading from one level to the next. The following is an example of one the skills in the Hold Groups competency — using a flip chart.

SKILL 3.1: USE FLIP CHART TO DISPLAY THE GROUP'S WORK

AWARENESS	APPLICATION	MASTERY
Displays group's work accurately • Do people read what is captured? Is it accurate? • Do I use the Context Statement, Effective Questions and Listen Fors to inform what is captured? • Does the speaker recognize what was said in what I captured? • Do I easily capture parallel conversations and accurately record decisions?	Displays group's work to focus on meeting results • Do my charts serve as a tool to recap work for summary? • Do I use techniques (color, underlining, symbols, spacing, lines) to highlight, track, and distinguish conversations? • Do people who were not in the conversation know its content from what is charted? • Do group members look at and refer to my charts?	Displays group's work to accelerate progress toward achieving meeting results • Do my charts support the building of proposals and making decisions? • Does my charting support synthesis and movement toward meeting results? • Do my charts support accountability for action during and after the meeting?

WHY ARE RBF SKILLS NEEDED?

Results Based Facilitation skills are needed because many meetings waste a lot of the time, energy, and talents of individuals who have good ideas and a desire to act on them. How many times have you had an experience like one of these?

• Sat through a meeting feeling frustrated and bored?

• Gritted your teeth in a meeting to keep from screaming because people have the same conversation over and over?

• Done everything you could to avoid going to a meeting because you knew your time would be better spent doing your own work in your own way?

• Checked out during a meeting and doodled, used your smartphone, read something, or daydreamed?

In fact, you may have noticed that frustrating and boring meetings can actually make a problem worse. Have you had any of the following experiences?

- People do not make effective decisions but instead struggle, spin, and make decisions that no one thinks are good because meeting fatigue causes people to say yes to almost anything.

- Group members do not achieve a greater understanding of each other or deepen their relationships but instead get angrier and become discouraged, doubtful that their problems will be solved.

- Some attendees do not contribute their insights, energy, or talents to a common goal, instead shutting down emotionally and intellectually and distancing themselves from each other and the work.

- People accept the desires and decisions of the few who promote their own solutions or agendas instead of putting forth and exploring ways to meet their own interests.

The premise of this book is that these experiences and feelings are the unintended consequences of meetings conducted in an unproductive way. Because of these negative consequences, unproductive meetings can be worse than no meeting at all.

One solution is to have no meetings or very few, thus limiting the pain. However, it is only by people working together creatively and effectively that many of the urgent and important issues in our organizational and community lives will be addressed.

WHAT ARE THE BENEFITS OF USING RBF SKILLS?

If you are experiencing these kinds of meetings, then RBF skills can help you to have productive meetings that move people from talking to taking action that produces results. People who must work together to address urgent and important issues need a way to hold productive meetings that lead to stronger outcomes, such as:

- stronger relationships
- clearer communication
- active participation
- shared learning
- exciting insights
- creative problem solving
- robust solution development
- helpful conflict resolution

> effective decision making

> commitment to action

> follow-through on commitments to action that produce results

HOW DO I DEVELOP THE RBF COMPETENCIES AND SKILLS?

The development of RBF skills begins by assessing where you are in your awareness of RBF. From that awareness, you can learn and enhance your skills through practice, reflection, application, and feedback. The development of RBF skills is personal and, by necessity, reflects where you are, who you are, and where you want to go. This journey has three stages:

BECOME AWARE OF SKILLS   →   APPLY THE SKILLS   →   MAKE THE SKILLS YOUR OWN

The path to mastery will be hard at times; it demands patience and discipline to understand the theory and integrate the skills. However, with practice, you will be able to contribute to people working well together, and you will begin to see how productive meetings help achieve good results in your organizations and communities.

HOW THIS BOOK SUPPORTS RBF SKILL DEVELOPMENT

This book is written for anyone interested in being a more effective meeting participant or in convening or facilitating meetings that lead to action and produce desired results. This book will help you to better understand the theory of RBF, become aware of the RBF competencies and skills, assess your current use of the skills, and practice your skills to produce results in meetings.

Throughout the book, reflective practice questions help you see the benefit of practicing the RBF methods. When you answer these questions, you are checking in to the work: discovering the connections between your own motivations, goals, and aspirations and the purpose of this book. A check-in involves aligning what you are looking for and what is offered. In other words, answering the question: *What's in it for me?*

CHECK-IN: A PROCESS TO FACILITATE CONNECTIONS TO A PERSON OR PEOPLE AND A TASK. WHEN CHECKED IN, PEOPLE ARE READY TO WORK TOGETHER.

Keeping your answers in mind as you develop your RBF skills will help you to achieve your own goals and get the benefits you desire.

The book is organized to support your unique learning style, offer you opportunities to reflect on your experience, help you adopt and practice skills, and help you learn and apply the theory. You may use this book in one of two ways: (1) read this book from cover to cover, learning the theory and practicing the skills over time, or (2) choose any section and use the contents of that section to meet an immediate need.

Let's take a look at the organization of Book One and find out how each chapter can contribute to your journey.

RBF Theory introduces the concepts underlying RBF, the RBF competencies, and the RBF developmental continuum.

RBF Practice describes the methods and approaches that support mastery of the RBF skills and competencies, including how to both give and receive skill-focused feedback.

Each of the four RBF foundation competencies are then explored in depth, enabling you to gain an awareness of the skills, assess your skill level, and find ways to practice and master the skills.

Competency 1: Hold Roles is the ability to be aware of and make choices about roles that contribute to achieving meeting results.

The Person-Role-System framework and the concept of boundaries of authority, role, and task (B/ART) enable you to consider your own role and that of others in meetings. The skills of this competency include defining and differentiating roles as they contribute to meeting results, understanding group dynamics to achieve meeting results, holding a neutral facilitator role, and giving work back to the group.

Competency 2: Hold Conversations is the ability to listen with openness, curiosity, and attentiveness to frame dialogues that achieve meeting results. The skills strengthen the quality of your listening and build your capacity to use Context Statements, Effective Questions, and an awareness of what to Listen For in conversations.

Competency 3: Hold Groups is the ability to support groups in having focused conversations that move to results. The Hold Groups competency includes the following skills:

- Using flip charts to document the work.

- Sequencing speakers, topics, and work to have one conversation at a time.

- Summarizing ideas, proposals, and decisions to support the ability to make decisions.

- Synthesizing ideas, meaning, and group dynamics to enable the move from talk to action.
- Checking in and checking out to support groups in beginning and ending their work together focused on results.

Competency 4: Hold 3R Meetings is the ability to use the 3R framework (Relationships, Resources, and Results) to design and facilitate meetings that move groups from talk to action. The 3R framework enables you to design meetings that build the relationships of meeting participants so that they can contribute their resources (what they know, what they care about, what they can do) to achieve results. Using these skills and the design templates provided lead to meetings that predictably move from talk to action.

Book One, Foundation Skills concludes with the **Pathway to Advanced Skills** that allows you to consider how best to continue your practice of the four foundation competencies because practice is an essential element of success.

You can practice the skills daily. Even though you may not be a facilitator, you are a meeting participant, an employee, a community member, or a family member. In each role, you can use RBF skills to listen appreciatively, clarify meaning, explore issues, create greater understanding, and (where appropriate) move to action. Practicing the skills as a meeting participant is both helpful in achieving results and one of the most effective ways to develop skills.

Once you've mastered the foundation skills, you may see the need for the advanced competencies to address more complex group dynamics, so this chapter provides a brief overview of the two advanced competencies (Hold Mental Models and Hold Action and Results) found in the next book in this series, *Results Based Facilitation: Book Two — Advanced Skills.*

Competency 5, Hold Mental Models is based on the premise that "problems cannot be solved by the same level of thinking that created them."[1] To stimulate new levels of thinking, this competency introduces a repertoire of mental models designed to support groups in clarifying issues, addressing challenges, and building relationships and making decisions to move from talk to action.

Competency 6, Hold Action and Results focuses on the skills and methods that enable groups of people to work together and make a measurable improvement in the well-being of populations they care about or serve.

You can find these two RBF books, other materials, and tools at *www.rbl-apps.com*. Many of the agendas, templates, and worksheets from the examples, exercises, and tips have been posted on the website.

In addition, support for the practice and development of the foundation and advanced skills can be found through the Results Based Facilitation Network. The mission of the network is to support the application and integration of Results Based Facilitation skills. You can connect to this network at *www.rbfnetwork.com*.

NOTE:

[1] Attributed to Albert Einstein.

THEORY:
THE FOUNDATIONS OF RBF

CONCEPTS IN THIS CHAPTER

THEORY OF ALIGNED
CONTRIBUTIONS

THREE HYPOTHESES OF
RESULTS BASED FACILITATION

RBF DEVELOPMENTAL
SEQUENCE: COMPETENCIES
AND ROLES

DIFFERENTIAL IMPACT: SAME
EXPERIENCE, DIFFERENT
REACTIONS

THE COLLABORATIVE WORK
CYCLE: ACCOUNTABILITY IN
ACTION

DEFINING MEETING RESULTS

In this chapter, you'll be introduced to key theories of Results Based Facilitation (RBF). These concepts will give you a foundation for learning the six competencies and 22 skills that make up the RBF approach.

≫ **Facilitate:** to make easier; to help bring about
– Merriam-Webster Online Dictionary

CONCEPTS IN THIS CHAPTER

RBF theory defines *meetings* as the engagement of people toward achieving a common purpose. The theory focuses on the *what* and *how* of the behaviors and relationships that move people to the actions that produce results. The RBF skill set is designed to make it easier for people to move from talk to action and achieve a common purpose together.

RBF is a collaborative leadership competency grounded in an emerging theory of change, the Theory of Aligned Contributions.[1] Preliminary evidence suggests that using RBF competencies contributes to leaders taking action together and, over time, holding themselves accountable for making a measurable improvement in organizational, neighborhood, or community results.[2]

THEORY OF ALIGNED CONTRIBUTIONS

The Theory of Aligned Contributions (TOAC) posits that people practicing a specific skill set are more likely to agree and take action toward a common result. Emerging evidence supports this theory.[3]

The TOAC informs the design and execution of meetings that predictably move leaders to holding themselves accountable for implementing aligned strategies at a scope and scale to measurably improve results. RBF meetings that implement the TOAC enable leaders to collaborate and be accountable for aligned action using the RBF skills. The research suggests that these skills — learned and practiced either by a meeting participant and/or an explicitly authorized facilitator — enable a group to own a common result, build the relationships necessary to work together to achieve the result, and contribute resources (knowledge, passion, influence, and capacity to act) to the common result.

With skills that develop alignment and accountability, over time groups can contribute to measurable improvement in program, neighborhood, and community results. The catalyst for action and results is the alignment of individual interests with group interest. In other words, what individuals want is aligned with the purpose of the group's work.

PRACTICE: RESULTS ALIGNMENT

> Consider meetings you have participated in. Take a moment to reflect on what the individual participants might have wanted from a meeting and the intended results of the meeting.
>
> • What was the degree of alignment between individual results and meeting results?
>
> • How did alignment or lack of alignment between individual results and meeting results impact the group's ability to move to action?

THE THREE HYPOTHESES OF RESULTS BASED FACILITATION

The work of alignment occurs through the interaction of individuals in meetings that move groups from talking to taking action. To support this work, *three RBF hypotheses* inform which competencies are included in the RBF skill set, how those competencies are defined, and what the sequence is for learning and applying the competencies.

HYPOTHESIS #1: THE WORK OF MEETINGS OCCURS THROUGH CONVERSATIONS.

Any meeting can be seen as a series of conversations of differing length. Within longer conversations are smaller conversations, each with an identifiable beginning, middle, and end.

Groups can have a series of conversations that create both meaning and movement toward action and results. A *group conversation* is defined as people listening to and talking about the same thing at the same time. Over time this practice leads to the following:

> » understanding and relationship building;
> » problem solving and conflict resolution; and
> » decision making and commitment to accountable, aligned actions.

HYPOTHESIS: A SUPPOSITION OR PROPOSED EXPLANATION MADE ON THE BASIS OF LIMITED EVIDENCE AS A STARTING POINT FOR FURTHER INVESTIGATION.

– OXFORD DICTIONARY

HYPOTHESIS #2: GROUP CONVERSATIONS CAN BE DESIGNED, PREPARED FOR, AND FLEXIBLY SUPPORTED BY SOMEONE WITH A SET OF LISTENING AND SPEAKING SKILLS.

Design, preparation, and interaction skills can be seen, named, practiced, and applied to all conversations. Each person in his or her role can practice these skills in conversations and can contribute to group ownership of the meeting purpose and the move to action. Learning and applying these skills start with awareness and choice about a role and a willingness to practice the skill set.

HYPOTHESIS #3: A PERSON HOLDING A NEUTRAL ROLE, USING A SET OF LISTENING AND SPEAKING SKILLS TO SUPPORT THE WORK OF A GROUP, CAN ACCELERATE THE WORK OF A GROUP.

Holding neutral in any role occurs when a person gives the work back to the group and does not use his or her authority to pursue a personal agenda. Holding neutral in a facilitator role is aided when the group authorizes specific tasks in support of achieving the articulated purpose of the group within commonly understood boundaries of time and place.

PRACTICE: THE WORK OF MEETINGS

- What are your assumptions about the work of meetings?
- What are your assumptions about the role and authority of a facilitator?

RBF DEVELOPMENTAL SEQUENCE: COMPETENCIES AND ROLES

Using skills in the neutral facilitator role is a central tenet of the three hypotheses. The theory holds that role awareness is a precondition for effective RBF skill development. From that awareness of role, people can begin to consciously participate in conversations in a way that moves groups from talk to action around a shared result. These roles can be participant, facilitator, supervisor, or meeting chair.

A developmental sequence that starts with role awareness illuminates for people how and when the specific competencies and skills can be deployed. The sequence supports the application of the skills in a variety of roles and circumstances, increasing the opportunities for practice and the places where the competencies and skills can provide value. The developmental sequence provides immediate benefit to the practitioner. If you can see your role and task, then you are more likely to find a way to take action and move toward results.

The developmental sequence (scaffolding) of the competencies follows:

1. **Hold Roles** — The first competency is to become aware of how people hold roles in meetings and choose to develop the skill of holding the neutral role (when beneficial) as a participant or as an authorized facilitator.

2. **Hold Conversations** — The second competency is to become aware that conversations are the focus of collaborative work and to choose to participate in conversations with an appreciation of and openness to other people and their points of view.

3. **Hold Groups** — The third competency is to become aware that groups are composed of diverse individuals. To understand each individual's perspectives, preferences, and interests, meeting participants must have one conversation at a time.

4. **Hold 3R Meetings** — The fourth competency is to become aware of the structure and process of conversations and to choose to master and apply methods that will help you design and execute meetings that produce results.

5. **Hold Mental Models** — The fifth competency is to become aware of the range of mental models available and choose to master and apply mental models that contribute to moving groups from talk to accountable, aligned action.

6. **Hold Action and Results** — The sixth and final competency is to become aware that in meetings groups can commit to aligned action and choose to work toward achieving results that lead to organizational or neighborhood results, and, ultimately, community results.

By using the six competencies in different roles, people can: (1) define the meeting results; (2) design and prepare for meetings; (3) support a group in achieving the defined meeting results or flexibly adopt different meeting results based on the work of the meeting and the meeting dynamics; (4) be accountable for progress toward meeting results; and (5) over time, know if the achieved meeting results lead to actions and results in organizations, neighborhoods, and communities.

PRACTICE: ROLES

- What role(s) do you typically play in meetings?
- What do you hope to achieve in your various roles by mastering these competencies?

DIFFERENTIAL IMPACT: SAME EXPERIENCE, DIFFERENT REACTIONS

For groups to own a common result, they need an understanding of how people in various roles may differ in their behavior and interests. RBF uses the concept of differential impact to illuminate how people engaged in the same conversation may have very different reactions to that common experience.

Using research and methods based on the Myers-Briggs Type Indicator (MBTI), RBF illuminates this *differential impact*. RBF integrates the approaches of the Person-Role-System[4] framework informed by Bion's work on whole-group relations[5] and the use of preferences to understand differences and similarities in how people take in information, make decisions, and interact with their environment.

The Person-Role-System (PRS) framework, combined with MBTI, provides a common language for exploring how people's unique characteristics influence their behavior in meetings and in their roles in organizational and community systems. The combination of the two approaches (illustrated in the figure on the next page) is useful in generating hypotheses about how individuals communicate in groups, make decisions, address change, and interact with each other in problem-solving and collaborative work. The top figure on the next page is "Person" and is an expanded view of what is included in "Person."

The integration of the two approaches — PRS and MBTI — is one example of how the concept of differential impact supports groups moving to alignment. As you can see, in addition to MBTI, there are many other dimensions of a person that will influence how that person picks up a role.

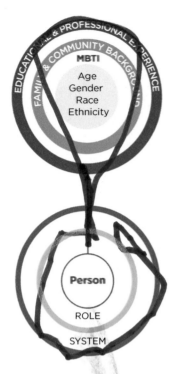

PERSON-ROLE-SYSTEM AND MBTI

The understanding of differential impact is deepened when insights from MBTI are combined with other factors such as age, gender, race, or professional background that may influence how a person in a role behaves in meetings. In addition, the sector in which a person works — e.g., public, nonprofit, for profit, etc. — can have a significant impact on a person's behavior in meetings.

MBTI informs people about their preferences; it is not about ability, skill, or competency. Type describes strengths and preferences. It is not judgmental or immutable. All preferences are valuable, and each person can use all preferences.

There are four sets of dichotomies associated with MBTI related to where people get their energy, how they take in information, how they make decisions, and how they orient themselves to the external world. The four dichotomies are as follows:

Extroversion (E) or Introversion (I)

An **E**xtrovert gains energy from the external world of people or activities.

An **I**ntrovert gains energy from the internal world of ideas, emotions, or impressions.

Sensing (S) or Intuition (N)

A **S**ensor prefers to use the five senses to gather data and note what is actual.

An i**N**tuitive gathers data, but prefers to constantly synthesize, extrapolate, and note what might be.

Thinking (T) or Feeling (F)

A **T**hinker prefers to organize information to make logical, objective decisions. The **T**hinker will step outside the problem to make decisions.

A **F**eeler prefers to organize information to make decisions in a personal, value-oriented way. The **F**eeler places him- or herself in the problem to make decisions.

Judging (J) or Perceiving (P)

A **J**udger prefers a planned or organized life.

A **P**erceiver prefers to be spontaneous and keep options open.

These four dichotomies provide the basis for the 16 MBTI types. One useful way to apply MBTI is to look at the combination of the Sensing or iNtuition preference with the Thinking or Feeling preference. The possible combinations — ST, SF, NF, and NT are called the four functional pairs because they say so much about how we function in life.[6]

MBTI provides a language for understanding one dimension of the dynamics of person-in-role that contributes to differential impact. For ease of reference, when using the lens of MBTI the RBF practice method uses the four functional pairs to understand differential impact. The four functional pairs provide an indication of what roles people may take in groups. An awareness of MBTI role preferences listed below illuminates differential impact at the person-in-role level. The table illustrates the roles and problem-solving and decision-making characteristics people may use in meetings.[7]

ROLES IN GROUPS AND CHARACTERISTICS FOR PROBLEM SOLVING AND DECISION MAKING

FUNCTIONAL PAIR	ROLE	CHARACTERISTICS
NF	Harmonizer/catalyst	Enthusiastic, insightful
SF	Caretaker/supporter	Sympathetic, friendly
ST	Stabilizer/operational excellence champion	Practical, matter of fact
NT	Visionary/architect	Logical, ingenious

THE COLLABORATIVE WORK CYCLE: ACCOUNTABILITY IN ACTION

RBF skills are specifically designed to move groups from talk to aligned, accountable action. The skills are deployed within an overarching mental model of what is possible and desirable *in* meetings in order to produce what is possible and desirable *between* meetings. The figure on the next page illustrates the mental model of the Collaborative Work Cycle.[8]

The Collaborative Work Cycle is RBF's mental model of how to use meetings to move from talk to accountable, aligned action between meetings, described further in the diagram on the next page.

A MENTAL MODEL IS AN EXPLANATION OF SOMEONE'S THOUGHT PROCESS ABOUT HOW SOMETHING WORKS IN THE REAL WORLD. MENTAL MODELS HELP SHAPE OUR BEHAVIOR AND DEFINE OUR APPROACH TO SOLVING PROBLEMS AND CARRYING OUT TASKS.

COLLABORATIVE WORK CYCLE

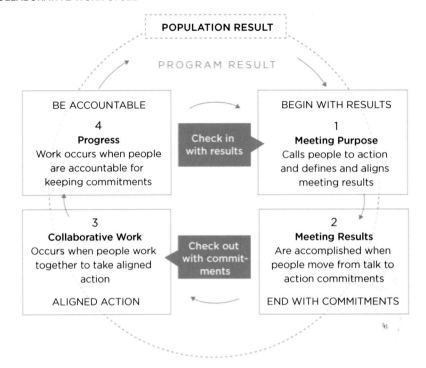

THE FOUR STEPS OF THE COLLABORATIVE WORK CYCLE

STEP	DESCRIPTION
1	**Enter a meeting with a focus on results.** RBF methods and competencies ensure that people come to meetings with a specific purpose and meeting results in mind. The purpose and meeting results connect the work of the meeting to the work outside the meeting.
2	**Leave a meeting with commitments to action.** RBF methods and competencies allow people to have conversations that move them from talk (information sharing, idea generation) to solving problems and resolving conflict to developing an action plan (strategy) to committing to action.
3	**Work to keep action commitments between meetings.** RBF methods and competencies support aligned action between meetings that focuses on execution of decisions and commitments made in meetings.
4	**Create accountability for action commitments between meetings.** RBF methods and competencies support the relationships and conversations that create accountability by intentionally assessing progress on action commitments made during meetings. The focus on accountability for aligned action replaces talking about results with doing the work of producing results.

- What is your orientation toward being accountable for action?
- Does accountability support you in moving to action?
- How does your orientation toward accountability for action influence how you participate in meetings?
- How does your approach to accountability for action inform how you facilitate meetings?

DEFINING MEETING RESULTS

The ability to make a link between meeting results and neighborhood or organizational results, and ultimately to community-wide results, is often missing. Yet, without this link, meetings can remain all talk and not lead to purposeful action. RBF requires a results framework and is compatible with most commonly used frameworks — such as the Balanced Scorecard.[9] RBF is particularly suitable for supporting the implementation of Friedman's Results Accountability Framework.[10] This framework is used in RBF to articulate the connection between what can be accomplished in meetings (meeting results) and actions between meetings.

MEETING RESULTS CONNECT TO PROGRAM AND POPULATION RESULTS

Accountability is about knowing what kind of difference you want to make and committing to making that difference. Naming the difference and being able to track your progress are essential to achieving results. This results focus requires an orientation to using information — both qualitative and quantitative — in a disciplined way.

Answering the following three performance-accountability questions developed by Friedman is helpful to making that connection between the work of meetings and the work between meetings that produces results.

- What did we do?
- How well did we do it?
- What difference did we make?

The Friedman framework is used in the next few pages to illustrate how clearly defined meeting results can contribute in a measurable way to clearly defined organizational and community-wide results. Answering the *"What difference did we make?"* question builds the bridge from talk to action as people hold themselves accountable for contributing to results in programs and communities.

The table on the next page illustrates how answering the three questions at the meeting level and taking action outside the meeting contribute to results. The example illuminates how meeting results can produce commitments to action, catalyze work, and contribute to more babies being born healthy in a community.

HOW MEETING RESULTS LEAD TO NEIGHBORHOOD OR ORGANIZATIONAL PROGRAM RESULTS

Meeting Results lead to action that produces effective programs and activities in neighborhoods: relationships strengthened, partners enrolled, information shared, data analyzed, ideas generated and issues explored, solutions developed, decisions and commitments made.

WHAT did we do? (how much/many?)	How WELL did we do it?
• Number of people at the meeting who have something to contribute to improving birth outcomes • Length of the meeting • Number of clearly defined meeting results	• Number of meeting results accomplished • Number of people who made commitments to action • Percentage of participants who say their interests in attending the meeting were met

What DIFFERENCE did we make?

Percentage who:

- say they have a new insight or understanding (knowledge)
- are using a common consensus decision-making method (skills)
- say they are more comfortable participating in discussions and speak more frequently (attitudes/behaviors)
- make commitments to take action (circumstance)
- say they kept commitments made at a prior meeting and took action outside the meeting to make a measurable contribution to a neighborhood or organizational program (circumstance)

AS A RESULT OF COMMITMENTS MADE AT THE MEETING, PARTICIPANTS TAKE ACTIONS THAT MAKE A DIFFERENCE.

Program and Population Results contribute to conditions of well-being for children, families, and adults in their communities: well-trained home visitors help pregnant women get prenatal care in the first trimester, families help pregnant women eat well and exercise, mothers in prenatal programs deliver healthy babies. Communities have a high rate of healthy babies in their population.

WHAT did we do? (how much/many?)	How WELL did we do it?
Number of: • nutrition workshops for pregnant mothers • new mothers enrolled in home-visiting programs • families provided with information on supporting pregnant women	*Percentage of:* • women who said they will follow nutritional guidelines provided during nutrition workshops • mothers in home-visiting programs who keep appointments • eligible mothers who use vouchers to purchase healthy food

What DIFFERENCE did we make?

Percentage of:

- pregnant mothers who know what exercise is appropriate during pregnancy (knowledge)
- pregnant mothers who can do exercises that prepare them for childbirth (skills)
- pregnant mothers motivated to exercise three times a week (attitudes/behaviors)
- mothers who give birth to a baby of healthy weight (circumstance)

Using MBTI Insights for Results Accountability

Using and applying the Friedman Results Accountability Framework in meetings requires adopting the framework and practicing language discipline. Some people find using the framework and language relevant and others do not; some find implementing the framework easy and others find it to be more difficult. To understand these differences, results accountability may be viewed through the lens of MBTI functional pairs. In the four examples below, what the person values and what they can contribute, may determine how they view results accountability, which, in turn, suggest different ways to engage each functional pair.

The **NF** (i**N**tuitive **F**eeler) takes on the role of harmonizer/catalyst and values and contributes to cordial relationships in groups. However, since results accountability often involves using data in the form of graphs and trend lines, NFs may have difficulty focusing on data points when they don't seem to tell a story. Here are some ways to more fully engage NFs:

Encourage them to imagine that all the data points of a trend line in a graph represent people's faces and stories — that the data *are* the people.

Emphasize that results accountability is about what people want to see in the world, and they can articulate their vision and passion about people and their well-being.

Highlight that partners are key to accomplishing results. Encourage NFs to think about who are or might be partners in accomplishing results. This approach appeals to NFs and motivates them to engage in discussions about whom to enroll in the work and how to communicate with people, especially around shared values.

Identify how NFs can contribute by creating the links among the people to make it apparent to all how achieving results might affect them and those they care about.

The **SF** (**S**ensing **F**eeling) takes on the role of caretaker/supporter and values supporting others. Because results accountability often involves using data and objective criteria to make decisions, SFs may find it hard to focus on the data and not be overly influenced by the opinions of people they care about. To more fully engage SFs:

Encourage them to use the information to devise practical solutions that will help the people they care about.

Emphasize that working toward a common result and directly addressing differences of opinion can lead to people getting what they want and need.

Highlight ways that SFs can interact in a collegial way to generate solutions. This approach appeals to them and motivates them to provide support to others and receive the sympathy, recognition, and support that fuels their energy.

Identify how SFs can contribute by ensuring that people have what they need to work well together.

 An **ST** (**S**ensing **T**hinking) takes on the role of stabilizer/operational excellence champion, often valuing and ensuring that execution steps are well defined. STs take accountability seriously, often at a personal level. As they look to achieve excellence, they often don't want to be accountable for things beyond their control, a feature of results accountability, which often involves individuals collectively holding themselves accountable for results that are unpredictable and uncertain, and that can't be controlled by one individual. They also can see a lot of downside risks to strategies. To more fully engage STs:

Encourage them to acknowledge the risk, to help figure out how to manage the risk, and to take an active role any implementation steps.

Emphasize that results accountability can be grounded in practical experience and/or evidence-based practice.

Highlight that they can help the group use a sequential process to ensure that work is organized and produces predictable, desired results.

Identify how STs can contribute to the group by sharing what has and what has not worked well in the past; they will engage more easily in discussions with a lot of specificity and concrete examples.

 An **NT** (i**N**tuitive **T**hinker) takes on the role of visionary/architect, often valuing and offering a big picture of how the parts make a whole. Results accountability involves taking the time to build relationships so that everyone understands the process and content in their own way. NTs often see the big picture and possibilities for action quickly, and, therefore, may be impatient. To more fully engage NTs:

Encourage NTs to see the importance of going slowly to build partnerships and shared understanding and to focus on the simplest thing that could work.

Emphasize that results accountability is one way for a group and NTs to envision a big picture that helps see part/whole relationships and uses results accountability.

Highlight that taking the time to establish a common purpose and results can provide the framework for strategic, decisive action.

Identify how NTs can contribute by making proposals about how everyone can help get results and what sequence of actions might move the group to results.

THEORY TO COMPETENCY

In the next section, you'll learn how to put RBF theory into practice. Practice methods are applied at the level of the 22 skills, which are organized into the six competencies. Each competency can be mapped to an element of the theory as shown below.

MAPPING OF THEORY ELEMENT TO THE COMPETENCY

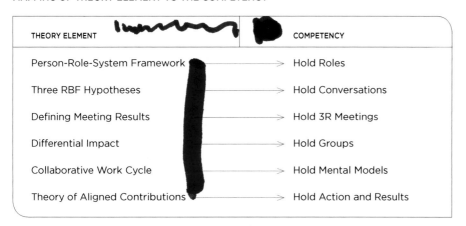

THEORY ELEMENT	COMPETENCY
Person-Role-System Framework	Hold Roles
Three RBF Hypotheses	Hold Conversations
Defining Meeting Results	Hold 3R Meetings
Differential Impact	Hold Groups
Collaborative Work Cycle	Hold Mental Models
Theory of Aligned Contributions	Hold Action and Results

NOTES:

[1] Pillsbury, Goddard-Truitt (Editor). *The Theory of Aligned Contributions.* Sherbrooke Consulting, Inc. 2007, 2010. Also see http://rbl-apps.com/TOAC.php.

[2] *Achieving Results with Collaboratives.* Research Brief. Fall 2011. The Results Based Leadership Collaborative at the University of Maryland School of Public Policy. www.publicpolicy.umd.edu/rblc.

[3] Littlefield, O'Brien, and Hersey. *Participant or Spectator: Non-profit Engagement in Multi-Sector Collaboratives.* American Society for Public Administration Conference. Baltimore, MD, March 2011.

[4] Green and Molenkamp. *The BART System of Group and Organizational Analysis.* 2005.

[5] Neuman, Holvinio, and Braxton. *Evolving a "Third Way" to Group Consultancy: Bridging Two Models of Theory and Practice.* Group Relations Reader 3. A K Rice Institute. 2003.

[6] www.myevt.com/teamdev/4-mbti-function-pairs.

[7] Hirsh and Hirsh. *Introduction to Type and Decision Making.* Consulting Psychologists Press. 2007.

[8] http://en.wikipedia.org/wiki/Mental_model.

[9] Kaplan and Norton. *The Balanced Scorecard.* Harvard Business Review Press. 1996. *The Balanced Scorecard* is a strategic planning and management system developed by Kaplan and Norton that aligns business activities to the vision and monitors organization performance against strategic goals.

[10] Friedman. *Trying Hard Is Not Good Enough.* Trafford Press. 2006. Friedman's framework is a results accountability approach used to define and achieve conditions of well-being for program and whole populations.

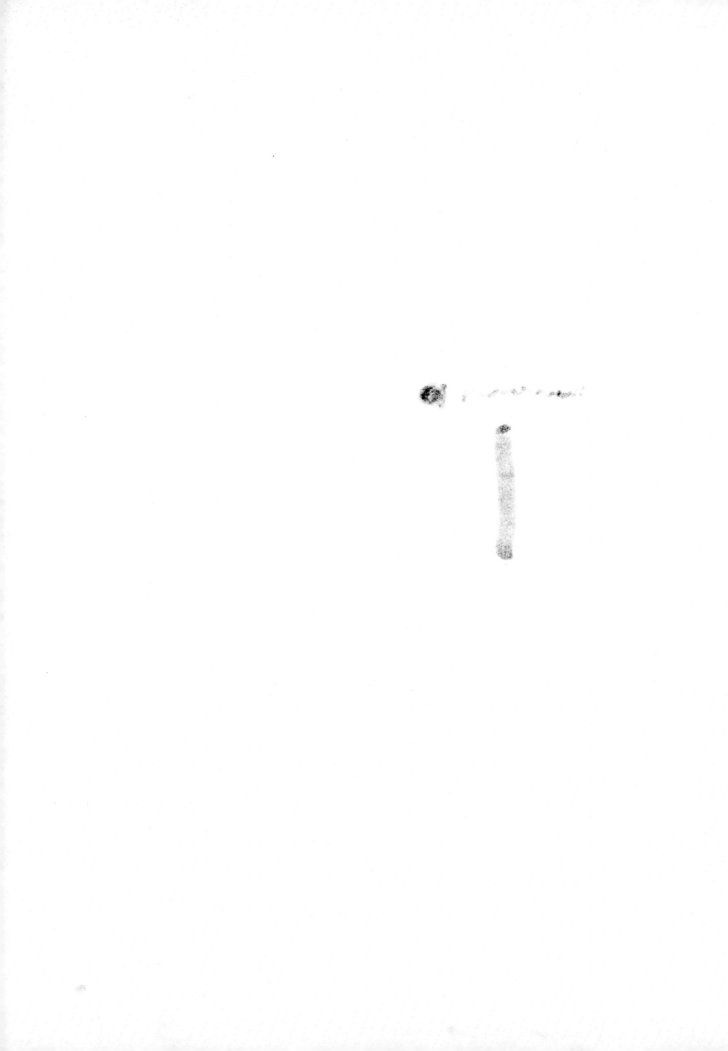

PRACTICE:
DEVELOPING RBF SKILLS

In this chapter, you'll be introduced to the RBF practice method and how to use feedback and coaching to develop RBF skills. These concepts will prepare you to practice RBF methods with assessments and exercises throughout the following chapters.

>   **Skill:** proficiency gained through deliberate and
    sustained practice

CONCEPTS IN THIS CHAPTER

RBF theory is competency based. Applying the theory requires practice that supports skill development.

The following methods enable the practitioner to develop mastery by deploying skills in a variety of roles:

- Exercises to develop the skills

- Reflective practice questions to support your development

- Tips and checklists on using the skills

- Opportunities for self-assessment of your skill level

- Examples of the differential impact of using the skill

- The opportunity to use an individual development plan for skill building

All of the above methods are useful in self-study. In addition, skill building in workshops can be supported by the use of physical objects such as *meme toys*,[1] enactments, feedback, and coaching.

Daily practice with attention to deploying the skill faithfully is the best predictor of skill mastery. Daily practice provides the requisite time on task[2] to achieve mastery.

THE EXPERIENTIAL LEARNING CYCLE

The RBF method grounds skill development in an *experiential learning cycle* that allows people to discover and learn what they need and want by reflecting on their own experiences, by seeing what their colleagues are doing, by using skills they want to learn, and by receiving feedback and coaching. The illustration below maps RBF methods to the experiential learning cycle.

THE EXPERIENTIAL LEARNING CYCLE

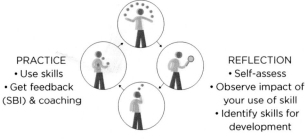

EXPERIENCE
• Observe skill
• Practice skill
• See meeting results

PRACTICE
• Use skills
• Get feedback
(SBI) & coaching

REFLECTION
• Self-assess
• Observe impact of
your use of skill
• Identify skills for
development

THEORY
• Apply theory
• Identify how to improve
skills based on theory

Skill development creates the discomfort of trying something new or doing something you already know in a new way. As you go through the experiential learning cycle, balance the *challenge* of learning with the *support* that allows you to experiment, try new things, and learn from doing. The term SBI in the figure refers to Situation, Behavior, Impact, a practice method of recording differential impact that is discussed later in this chapter.

RBF COMPETENCY ASSESSMENT CONTINUUM

Self-assessment is a critical step in the experiential learning cycle. The RBF competency assessment continuum, with its three levels for each of the 22 RBF skills, helps the practice lead to improvement. These levels are described below (you will see the icons repeated with the practice opportunities included in each chapter).

RBF SKILL LEVELS

Developing awareness begins with an initial understanding of the concepts — and a rudimentary command of the skill. You are developing awareness when you can see and *name the skill.*	**Begin by seeing**
Applying the skill involves a deeper and broader understanding of the skill and the ability to use the skill well in various situations. You are applying the skill when you can *do it consciously.*	**Move to doing**
Mastering the skill occurs when you have internalized it and demonstrated the ability to consistently integrate the skill in most situations. You have mastered the skill when you have made it your own, and the skill is now *a part of who you are.*	**Make it part of your being**

The practice method is grounded in self-assessment of skills. Self-assessment plays the dual role of creating more awareness of the skill and establishing a baseline. In the process, you use a series of questions to assess whether you are developing awareness of the skill, applying the skill, or mastering the skill.

The initial self-assessment provides a starting point or foundation for skill development and practice. In this initial assessment, some of the skills and competencies will be familiar, and some will not. You may currently be using some of these skills but either use a different name for the skill or do not consciously consider that what you do is a named skill. As you go through the learning cycle for each of the skills, your self-assessment will become more informed and your practice more focused.

PRACTICE: SELF-ASSESSMENT

- Where have you used self-assessment to build skills?
- What was your reaction to doing a self-assessment using the RBF Competency Assessment?

The skills are organized into the six competencies listed on the next page. A competency is the ability to hold a particular skill set, behavior, or way of being and thinking. You hold a competency when you can maintain a desired or accustomed level of mastery. RBF skills are sequenced to *scaffold* the experiential learning.[3]

Take the opportunity to experience this aspect of the practice method by using the table to do an initial self-assessment of your skill level. The assessment allows you to gauge the current level of skill, receive and give feedback, and identify next steps for practice in Individual Development Plans (IDPs).

COMPETENCY ASSESSMENT OF RBF SKILLS

RBF FOUNDATION SKILLS AND COMPETENCIES (BOOK ONE)	SKILL LEVEL/CONTINUUM		
	AWARENESS	APPLICATION	MASTERY
HOLD ROLES: Be aware of and make choices about roles that contribute to achieving results.			
Use B/ART to define and differentiate roles as they relate to meeting results			
Use B/ART to understand group dynamics and achieve meeting results			
Hold neutral facilitator role			
Give the work back to the group			
HOLD CONVERSATIONS: Listen with openness, curiosity, and attentiveness to frame dialogues that achieve meeting results.			
Demonstrate appreciative openness			
Use Context Statements, Effective Questions, and Listen Fors			
HOLD GROUPS: Support groups to hold focused conversations that move to results.			
Use flip chart to display the group's work			
Sequence			
Summarize			
Synthesize			
Check in and check out			
HOLD 3R MEETINGS: Use the 3R framework to design and facilitate meetings that move groups from talk to action.			
Use the 3Rs to design the meeting			
Use the 3Rs in the meeting to achieve results			
RBF ADVANCED SKILLS AND COMPETENCIES (BOOK TWO)			
HOLD MENTAL MODELS: Use a repertoire of perspectives that contribute to achieving meeting results.			
Use proposal-based decision making to move from talk to action			
Use conversations to develop convergence			
Name and address barriers to convergence			
Make and help others make action commitments			
Be and help others be accountable for action commitments			
Observe and respond to group dynamics			
Assess and address conflict			
HOLD ACTION AND RESULTS: Make a difference in programs and community populations.			
Be accountable in role for contributions to results			
Use RBF skills to work collaboratively to accelerate progress toward results			

THE STAGES OF COMPETENCE

For most people, assessing skills in a new way or in a new area of learning using unfamiliar terms can be uncomfortable, confusing, and frustrating. For example, in completing the RBF Competency Assessment, you may discover names for things that you did not consciously think of as skills. Or perhaps you may feel validated in skills you have been practicing for years or vulnerable that you may not have mastered certain skills.

The assessment process, though uncomfortable, is intended to evoke these reactions and create an awareness of where you are in your development. The *stages of competence* illustrated here describe the psychological states experienced when progressing from incompetence to competence.[4]

THE STAGES OF COMPETENCE

Unconscious Competence
Extensive time on task internalizes skill.
The individual performs the skill without concentrating too deeply.

Conscious Competence
Repetitive practice, feedback, coaching, and reflection build skill.
The individual knows how to do something; using the skill requires conscious effort.

Conscious Incompetence
Practice offers opportunities to work toward competence.
The individual recognizes the need to do something but is not yet addressing that need.

Unconscious Incompetence
Experience triggers awareness of a need for a new skill.
The individual neither knows how to do something nor recognizes the need to do something.

FROM AWARENESS TO MASTERY

Based on your assessment, you may identify a skill or skills that you would like to learn. Take a moment to think about the times in your life when you discovered a new skill that you wanted to learn. Think about your experiences on the path to mastery and answer the questions in the practice on the next page.

Consider a time when you mastered a new skill.

- What were the psychological and emotional costs and benefits of learning that skill?

- What helped you develop awareness of the skill?

- How were you able to apply the skill or skills?

- What helped you master the skill?

- Have you maintained the skill?

- What are some insights that might help you learn a new skill?

THE DIFFERENTIAL IMPACT OF LEARNING PREFERENCES IN SKILL DEVELOPMENT

Using personality type indicators (MBTI) supports more effective skill development and can help us understand differential impact — how the same behavior will have a different impact on different people. For example, you'll recall that MBTI makes a distinction between sensing and intuition.[5]

- Sensors (**S**s) are people with a preference for taking in information first through their five senses — what they actually see, hear, touch, taste, smell.

- Intuitives (**N**s) are people who first take in the big picture or symbolic meaning and may not notice specific details.

MBTI highlights differences in how people prefer to make decisions by distinguishing between two orientations: feeling and thinking.

- Thinkers (**T**s) are people with a preference for making decisions by first applying external criteria; they tend to focus on logic and analysis.

- Feelers (**F**s) are people with a preference for making decisions by first considering how the decision will affect them and those they care about; they tend to focus on personal values and priorities.

Ts and **F**s may come to the same decision. However, they will come at it from a different perspective. **T**s tend to focus more on impersonal facts and criteria, and **F**s focus on personal concerns and the people involved.

The following table presents an example of how using the learning styles of the four functional pairs (SF, ST, NT, NF) demonstrate differential impact. The table also provides insights about how different approaches to skill building can contribute to mastery.

CHANGE IS THE END RESULT OF ALL TRUE LEARNING. CHANGE INVOLVES THREE THINGS: FIRST, DISSATISFACTION WITH SELF — A FELT VOID OR NEED; SECOND, A DECISION TO CHANGE — TO FILL THE VOID OR NEED; AND THIRD, A CONSCIOUS DEDICATION TO THE PROCESS OF GROWTH AND CHANGE — THE WILLFUL ACT OF MAKING THE CHANGE; DOING SOMETHING.

– UNKNOWN

PAIR	IS INTERESTED IN	LEARNS BEST BY	NEEDS	WANTS FROM TEACHER
SF	Facts about real things; useful, practical information about everyday activities	Doing hands-on activities with others	Facts; straight, sequential instructions; frequent, friendly interaction; approval	Sympathy; support; individual recognition
NF	New ideas about how to understand people; symbolic and metaphorical activities	Imagining and/or creating with others; writing	General direction, with freedom to do it their own creative way; frequent positive feedback	Sense and share warmth, enthusiasm, humor; individual recognition
ST	Useful, practical information about how to do things well	Putting ideas into practice	Precise, step-by-step instructions; logical presentation backed by solid facts	Be treated fairly
NT	Theories and global explanations about why the world works the way it does	Categorizing, analyzing, applying logic	A big problem to solve or an intellectual challenge, then to be allowed to work it out	Be treated with respect; competence

SUPPORTING SKILL DEVELOPMENT WITH FEEDBACK AND COACHING

In the experiential learning cycle, feedback and coaching are the primary methods for skill development. RBF's method of giving and receiving feedback to accelerate skill development is called *Situation, Behavior, Impact* or SBI.[6] RBF also makes a distinction between feedback and coaching. The following section defines feedback, SBI, and coaching.

RBF FEEDBACK

Feedback is information about behavior that is given in the present so that it may influence the way people behave in the future. Remember that advice is not feedback. Advice is an opinion that is offered as something that is worthy to be followed, i.e., counsel. Usually advice is about "shoulds." *Advice* is often unsolicited, unappreciated, and ignored. In contrast:

- Feedback is about observation.

- Feedback is timely.

- Feedback is specific.

- Feedback includes the impact created, such as reactions and perceptions.

- Feedback describes but does not judge.

- Feedback is different from criticism or praise — it is not evaluative.

Some examples:

feedback: "When you started the meeting, the question on the chart was clearly written, but when you read the question your voice was so low that I couldn't hear you."

criticism: "You communicated poorly."

praise: "You communicated well."

Feedback involves giving information that can help the people receiving it make choices about their own performance without your telling them what to do.

Receiving feedback is best done by focusing on hearing it clearly, expressing appreciation for the information, then giving yourself time to process what you have heard before deciding what to do with it.

When you receive feedback, do not try to explain what you were doing or why — accept the feedback as it is offered. Keep in mind that one person's feedback reflects differential impact. As you learned in our discussion of differential impact earlier in the chapter, two people experiencing the same behavior from you may react differently. With this awareness, you can choose how or whether to use the feedback to inform your practice and development.

SBI: A MODEL OF CONSTRUCTIVE FEEDBACK

To develop RBF skills, you will use a specific method of feedback — Situation, Behavior, Impact (SBI) — to provide feedback to others and to request feedback from others. SBI provides information about the impact of the behaviors associated with the use of RBF skills. SBI focuses the practice on skill improvement and illuminates differential impact.

S DESCRIBE THE SITUATION

Specify the situation in which the behavior occurred. Describe when and where the behavior occurred. The more specific details you can use in bringing the situation to mind, the clearer your feedback will be.

Example: "When you turned your back in order to flip chart during the discussion on norms..."

Not: "When you were facilitating..."

B DESCRIBE THE BEHAVIOR (NOT AN INTERPRETATION OF THAT BEHAVIOR)

Behavior is a person's action; behavior is described using verbs (action words).

Example: "You lost eye contact with the group for several minutes."

Not: "Turning your back was poor practice."

Impact statements offer candid (authentic, accurate) feedback of your emotional response and how that emotion affected your participation in the conversation.

> *Example:* "When you turned your back in order to flip chart during the discussion on norms, you lost eye contact with the group for several seconds. During that time, everyone was speaking at once, and I couldn't figure out how to get my voice heard. It made me feel unappreciated, and I withdrew from the conversation."
>
> *Not:* "The conversation fell apart."

SBI Practice Method

The practice method that accelerates the development of RBF skills is as follows:

- Skill practice followed by appreciative self-assessment.
- Feedback using SBI, shared by those who experienced the skill practice.

For the method to be effective, the practitioner is challenged to listen deeply and not question or contest the feedback but use it to develop greater awareness of differential impact.

The following is an example of how the SBI practice method can illuminate the differential impact of the same behavior on two participants:

Situation: You were checking to see who wanted to speak at the beginning of the meeting.

Behavior: You said to Ann, *"You haven't raised your hand; however, I may be reading something from your expression — do you want to speak?"*

Impact Statement (from Ann): *"I appreciated being asked. I realized I did have something to say and was comfortable saying it."*

Impact Statement (from another participant): *"I got concerned when you asked Ann if she wanted to speak. I wasn't ready to share and was anxious you would also ask me."*

SBI Feedback

The following is the form used to provide SBI feedback in RBF workshops. It is also appropriate for use in coaching and peer feedback environments.

FACILITATOR OBSERVED: DATE/TIME:

YOUR NAME: MBTI TYPE:

YOUR ROLE DURING THE FACILITATION*:

Situation (when and where):

Behavior (specific description of what you observed the facilitator say or do):

Impact (the impact on you in role: what you felt or thought in response to the situation and behavior of the facilitator and how it affected your participation):

* The role you have in a group or in relation to the other group members and/ or the facilitator informs how you experience another person's behavior. For example, when in a supervisor role, you may be more sensitive to behavior that might challenge your authority than when you are in a peer role.

RBF COACHING

RBF coaching is specific to the RBF skills and is only done with permission from the person receiving the coaching. Coaching supplements self-assessment and SBI to accelerate skill building. Coaching is best done by those who have reached mastery in the RBF skills and have experience using the RBF coaching approach and practice methods.

RBF coaching is about challenging and supporting people, giving them the gift of the coach's attention and focusing on their skill development. The person being coached must give permission for the coach to interrupt, intervene, and provide specific guidance and methods of practice. Coaching is about behaviors and is up close and personal, sharing observation and guidance about voice, body, affect, and specific skills. It can include labeling, inquiry, dialogue, direct instruction, and behavior modeling (by the coach).[7]

The Coaching Model as Applied to RBF Skill Building

The RBF coach listens and observes. He or she focuses on specific skills and how the skills are used (message and medium). The coach contrasts what is being observed with the ideal of what the skill looks like at the mastery level, an approach sometimes called the coach's point of view.

The coach provides opportunities for reflection that create awareness of what changes the practitioner must make to build the skill. The coach uses positive feedback to reinforce the practitioner's behavior changes associated with growing mastery of the skill. The coach also provides direct instruction, modeling of the skill, and encouragement of skill practice.

Even if you don't have access to a qualified RBF coach, you can solicit SBI feedback in written or oral form from coworkers or meeting participants. You can also observe the impact of your skills to guide your practice and skill development.

WHAT YOU DO SPEAKS SO LOUDLY THAT I CANNOT HEAR WHAT YOU SAY.

- RALPH WALDO EMERSON

USING THIS BOOK FOR COMPETENCY AND SKILL ASSESSMENT AND DEVELOPMENT

The RBF practice method is incorporated into each of the skill-building chapters in this book. Each chapter includes an introduction to the competencies and skills, followed by a table that provides skill assessment questions, exercises for developing the skills at each level, a Participant Practice Guide to support day-to-day skill practice, and an opportunity to commit to your next steps of skill development. The method begins with assessing your current skill level at one of three levels discussed — Awareness, Application, and Mastery:

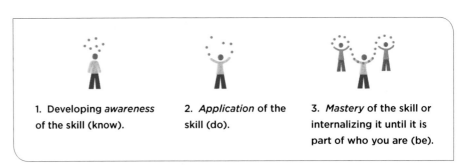

1. Developing *awareness* of the skill (know).

2. *Application* of the skill (do).

3. *Mastery* of the skill or internalizing it until it is part of who you are (be).

Each of the skills discussed in this book has the familiar three levels of mastery. The table below shows an example of a skill in the Hold Groups competency. Each skill level contains a statement describing what the skill at that level looks like, followed by questions to help you self-assess. The arrows below show progress along the continuum.

SKILL 3.4: SYNTHESIZE

AWARENESS	APPLICATION	MASTERY
Briefly states the meaning of short conversations • *Do I listen for the central meaning of the conversation and state that concisely?* • *Do I use basic methods of synthesis (comparison, themes, part/whole connections) in listening for and concisely stating where the group is in their work?*	Integrates and briefly states the meaning of a number of conversations or longer conversations • *Does the group affirm my synthesis and use it to move forward to meeting results?* • *Do I use images and symbolism to help the group own the results of a whole meeting?*	Integrates and briefly states the meaning for a whole meeting • *Does my synthesis accelerate the group's work?* • *Does the group use my synthesis to move to action?*

Developing skill mastery requires intention and practice. Because most people spend more time in meetings as participants rather than as facilitators, Participant Practice Guides are provided for each skill and give examples of how to deploy RBF skills. The examples range from no risk to high risk, as shown in the example in the table below. The no- and low-risk uses of the skill are appropriate when you are initially developing comfort and confidence in using the skill. As you become more comfortable, confident, and experienced in deploying the RBF skills, the medium- to high-risk examples may become possible for you. As you use the skills daily, what might be high risk today may be low risk tomorrow.

PARTICIPANT PRACTICE GUIDE 3.4:
SYNTHESIZE

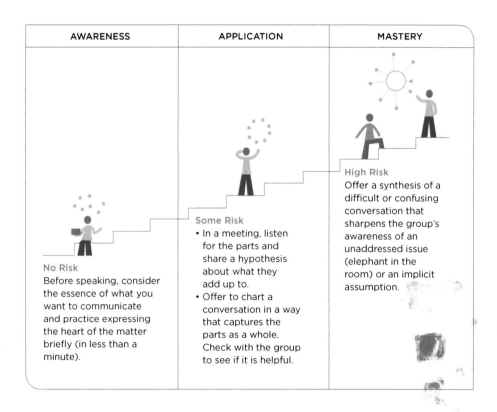

AWARENESS	APPLICATION	MASTERY
No Risk Before speaking, consider the essence of what you want to communicate and practice expressing the heart of the matter briefly (in less than a minute).	**Some Risk** • In a meeting, listen for the parts and share a hypothesis about what they add up to. • Offer to chart a conversation in a way that captures the parts as a whole. Check with the group to see if it is helpful.	**High Risk** Offer a synthesis of a difficult or confusing conversation that sharpens the group's awareness of an unaddressed issue (elephant in the room) or an implicit assumption.

In addition to the Participant Practice Guides, exercises and tips provided for each skill can be used to strengthen your skills in the participant role.

SKILL BUILDING: USING AN INDIVIDUAL DEVELOPMENT PLAN

This book uses the *Individual Development Plan* (IDP) to support skill development. The IDP enables the practitioner to choose the specific skills to develop and then decide what to practice and how. Following is an example of an IDP for the skill of flip charting in the Hold Groups competency. An IDP for each competency can be found in Appendix A.

EXAMPLE IDP FOR THE SKILL OF FLIP CHARTING

SKILL/PRESENT LEVEL	WHAT WILL I PRACTICE TO BUILD SKILL?	WHERE AND HOW WILL I PRACTICE DAILY?	WHAT IS THE DESIRED IMPACT OF IMPROVING THE SKILL?
Charting — my handwriting is not legible Level: awareness	The formation and spacing of letters	Place a flip chart in my office to chart key decisions from conversations with subordinates, pay attention to using the flat edge of the marker and making the letters 2.5 inches high	My subordinates will be able to easily read the decisions and we will refer to them to ensure execution. I will both observe the impact of my charting and request SBI from my subordinates about the usefulness of my charting.

Your skill assessment points to the skills that need strengthening. To accelerate development, the IDP encourages skill repetition and integration of practice into daily work. The IDP encourages you to design your daily skill practice to build mastery. Part of the development includes being clear about the desired impact of the higher skill level. By specifying this impact, you can use your practice experiences to assess your progress and continue toward mastery.

MBTI learning preferences illuminate differential impact and provide insight about how and what might be helpful in creating the IDP. For example:

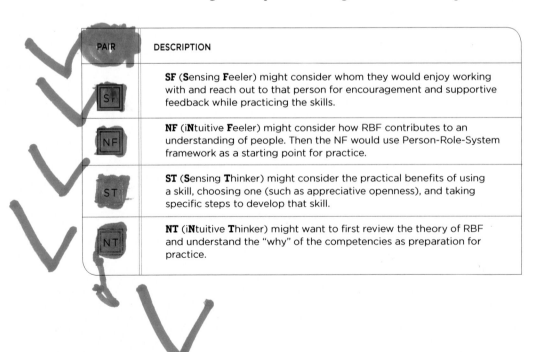

PAIR	DESCRIPTION
SF	**SF** (**S**ensing **F**eeler) might consider whom they would enjoy working with and reach out to that person for encouragement and supportive feedback while practicing the skills.
NF	**NF** (i**N**tuitive **F**eeler) might consider how RBF contributes to an understanding of people. Then the NF would use Person-Role-System framework as a starting point for practice.
ST	**ST** (**S**ensing **T**hinker) might consider the practical benefits of using a skill, choosing one (such as appreciative openness), and taking specific steps to develop that skill.
NT	**NT** (i**N**tuitive **T**hinker) might want to first review the theory of RBF and understand the "why" of the competencies as preparation for practice.

NOTES:

[1] In this context a meme toy is a physical object that makes a behavior or skill easier to use in practice. It is a correlate to stress toys that many facilitators use in meetings. You can find RBF-related meme toys on the rbl-apps.com website.

[2] In *Outliers*, Gladwell posits that 10,000 hours of practice are associated with mastery in a variety of disciplines.

[3] Scaffolding the learning represents an intentional developmental sequence of learning.

[4] http://en.wikipedia.org/wiki/Four_stages_of_competence

[5] Adapted from *Introduction to Type: A Guide to Understanding Your Results on the Myers-Briggs Type Indicator*. Sixth Edition by Isabel Briggs Myers. Consulting Psychologists Press, Inc.

[6] A description of the more general use of SBI, as originally developed by the Center for Creative Leadership, can be found at www.ccl.org/leadership/pdf/community/SBIJOBAID.pdf.

[7] Pillsbury. *RBF Coaching*. Sherbrooke Consulting, Inc. 2009.

HOLD ROLES

DEFINITION: BE AWARE OF AND MAKE CHOICES ABOUT ROLES THAT CONTRIBUTE TO ACHIEVING RESULTS

> ALONE WE CAN DO SO LITTLE; TOGETHER WE CAN DO SO MUCH.
>
> – HELEN KELLER

CONCEPTS IN THIS CHAPTER

THE PERSON-ROLE-SYSTEM FRAMEWORK

THE BOUNDARIES OF AUTHORITY, ROLE, AND TASK (B/ART)

SKILLS FOR THIS COMPETENCY

1.1 USE B/ART TO DEFINE AND DIFFERENTIATE ROLES AS THEY RELATE TO MEETING RESULTS

1.2 USE B/ART TO UNDERSTAND GROUP DYNAMICS AND ACHIEVE MEETING RESULTS

1.3 HOLD NEUTRAL FACILITATOR ROLE

1.4 GIVE THE WORK BACK TO THE GROUP

In this chapter, you have the opportunity to explore and understand RBF's first foundation competency: Hold Roles. The Hold Roles competency provides the skill set needed to choose how to work with others in a variety of roles and how to hold the role of a neutral facilitator: a person holding the neutral role can accelerate the work of the group. The chapter explains why the Hold Roles competency is important, what skills you need to develop and how to apply and practice the skills to achieve mastery of the competency.

> » **Role:** the function assumed or part played by a person in a particular situation

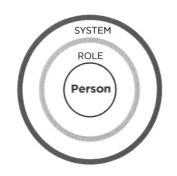

PERSON-ROLE-SYSTEM FRAMEWORK

THE PERSON-ROLE-SYSTEM FRAMEWORK

For all the RBF skills to be useful and worth learning, you need to see how, when, and to what end those skills can be used effectively in different roles. This understanding is a first step toward mastery of the Hold Roles competency. The awareness of the person in a role and his or her role in a system is the underlying concept of the Person-Role-System framework.

In the Person-Role-System framework, a person's choices and actions are influenced by who they are as a unique individual and by roles they play (consciously and unconsciously) in systems. This concept is illustrated in the figure on the left.

For example, one person might simultaneously be a father or mother in the family system, a member of the neighborhood watch in the local community system, a supervisor of a unit in an organizational system, and member of a cross-sector collaborative in a community-wide system.

THE BOUNDARIES OF AUTHORITY, ROLE, AND TASK (B/ART)

With awareness of the Person-Role-System comes the ability to see that in different roles people have different tasks with different authorities to do those tasks. The figure on the next page illustrates the "sweet spot" of alignment — the clear boundary of a person's authority and task for a specific role and circumstance.[1,2]

For example, a father or mother's task and authority relate to raising children. A neighborhood watch member's task and authority relate to the safety of the neighborhood. A supervisor's task and authority are to manage a unit's performance.

Notice that in each instance the task — parenting, neighborhood volunteer safety patrol, management and oversight — *defines* the necessary authority to operate in that role and also *sets the limits* of that authority. For example: Parents are authorized to parent only their own children (unless they have explicit permission to parent other children). A neighborhood watch member is authorized to patrol only his or her neighborhood. A supervisor is authorized to manage only the people in his or her unit.

These limits create boundaries for authority, role, and task. Similarly, meeting participants have roles (formal and informal, conscious and unconscious) that they play. These roles vary by the type of meeting and who the other participants are.

TASK: A PIECE OF WORK TO BE DONE OR UNDERTAKEN

B/ART provides a lens for understanding group dynamics and the relationships of group members to each other. Each person is unique; however, each person's behaviors in a group are influenced by the roles played within formal and informal systems and individual preferences and experiences.

For example, a person's MBTI can influence the way he or she is perceived in roles or picks up roles in systems. Similarly, people may express themselves differently depending on the role held in a particular moment. The same person might have a different demeanor as a supervisor with subordinates than when with their peers from another organization. Further, the expected behavior of a supervisor might look and feel different in different systems.

While RBF skills can be used in many roles, using the skills easily and well requires making a conscious choice in the context of a specific meeting, conversation, or body of work. Body of work refers to the broad spectrum of tasks you are authorized to undertake in your multiple roles. For example, a unit supervisor or office director has the ongoing body of work of delegating and assessing performance. A consultant's body of work consists of client engagements of different duration and varying scope. A task force leader may have a project as a body of work that is temporary and/or time limited.

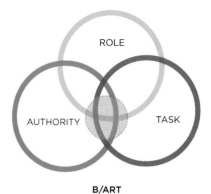

B/ART

SKILLS FOR THIS COMPETENCY

SKILL 1.1: USE B/ART TO DEFINE AND DIFFERENTIATE ROLES

The B/ART lens enables you to understand group dynamics from a Person-Role-System and role-in-system perspective. The following table defines the skill and provides questions to help assess your current skill level.

AWARENESS	APPLICATION	MASTERY
Understands the concept of B/ART • *Do I understand the Person-Role-System framework?* • *Do I know and can I name my own B/ART in my daily work and in meetings?*	Consciously establishes role in groups • *Do I comfortably name my role in meetings?* • *Do I understand the differences in my various roles?*	Uses awareness of B/ART to contribute to meeting results and move from talk to action • *Do I consciously make choices to hold my stated role during a meeting?* • *Do I use my understanding of B/ART to align my actions with others to achieve results?*

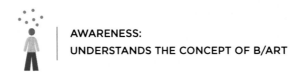

AWARENESS:

UNDERSTANDS THE CONCEPT OF B/ART

You are aware of this skill when:

• *you understand the Person-Role-System framework.*

• *you know and can name your own B/ART in daily work and in meetings.*

Every individual plays a number of roles in meetings and in organizations. The figure illustrates the overlapping nature of the roles. For example, you may have a consulting role in an organization with authority to offer advice and information in your area of expertise.

However, if the work of a particular meeting is not in your area of expertise, you would be present in the role of a participant. Your role defines your task and your authority to accomplish your task. Understanding the boundaries of task and authority enables you to hold your role in meetings.

Analyzing different roles helps deepen your understanding of how to apply the concept of B/ART. The Role Analysis Matrix on the next page defines the role, task, boundary, and authority of seven roles: participant, convener, neutral results based facilitator, trainer, consultant, supervisor, and meeting chair. The neutral facilitator column is highlighted to serve as a comparison to the B/ART of the other roles. Note the differences among all seven roles. Also compare each role to that of the neutral facilitator, which helps you to more easily learn to hold the neutral role.

Each role contains a role description and examples of the tasks and authority for that role. Most people shift roles many times a day and unconsciously reorient their behavior and interactions to each situation.

PRACTICE: B/ART

The intention of this reflection and analysis is to make the process *conscious* and to provide labels for the distinctions in B/ART.

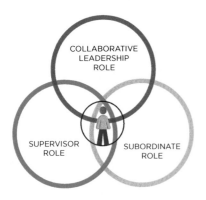

COLLABORATIVE LEADERSHIP ROLE

SUPERVISOR ROLE

SUBORDINATE ROLE

A PERSON IN MULTIPLE ROLES

Review the Role Analysis Matrix table, shown on the following page.

• What roles do you play in meetings?

Review the boundaries of authority and task for that role.

• How similar is that description to the way you currently hold that role?

• Are there any insights that might influence how you will hold that role in the future?

BOUNDARY OF AUTHORITY, ROLE, AND TASK	MEETING PARTICIPANT	MEETING CONVENER	NEUTRAL RESULTS BASED FACILITATOR	TRAINER	CONSULTANT	SUPERVISOR	MEETING CHAIR
ROLE DESCRIPTION Selected, held, and made clear to others for the meeting or conversation	A member of the group with a point of view	A host who calls the group together	A supporter of the group's meeting results and purpose	An expert imparting knowledge	An advisor providing information and recommenda-tions	A leader making decisions, delegating tasks, and holding accountability	A moderator presiding over the meeting and ensuring that the agenda is accomplished
TASK Overall	To engage in conversations, make proposals and decisions within their B/ART	To organize, open, and close the meeting	To facilitate the group in making its decisions	To teach and assess trainees	To meet client expectations regarding deliverables	To direct work and be accountable for implementation	To convene the meeting, hold the agenda, and cast the deciding vote in case of a tie
BOUNDARY OF ROLE AND TASK Time, event, location, purpose	Specific to the meeting(s), consider: who invited you, why you are there, who else is there, and the purpose of the meeting	Specific to the meeting(s), consider the purpose of the meeting, whose purpose it is, and your relationship to the participants	Specific to the meeting(s), consider who invited you to hold the role, their relationship to the meeting purpose, your relationship to the people, and purpose of the meeting	Specific to the course or workshop, consider what your credentials or qualifications are, what is at stake for the trainees, and your authority to assess performance	Specific to the engagement as defined by the client, consider what the statement of work is, who holds accountability for perform-ance, and your relationship to the client	Specific to the organization, consider to whom you are accountable, for what tasks, and who is accountable to you	The scheduled meetings of the board and/or committees
SOURCE AND SCOPE OF AUTHORITY To accomplish tasks: make decisions, take action, hold accountability	From the group represented, from the participant, or from the group — specific to the tasks of the meeting May share in decision making, depending on B/ART (theirs and others)	From the sponsoring organization or group or from the convener Makes decisions about content, timing, invitees, and the meeting purpose	From the group of meeting participants Facilitates the group in making its own decisions	From the credentialing or authorizing body in trainer's field of expertise Makes decisions about course content and trainee performance	From the client and from consultant's expertise Makes decisions about what to present at meetings and recommends decisions to the client	From the organization Makes decisions about tasks, assignments, next steps, and about time, content, and process of meetings	From the articles of incorporation or other documented agreements defining purpose and membership Makes decisions about agenda, process, and substance

Take a minute and reflect on the questions below about Person-Role-System to illuminate the interaction of these factors in how you and others hold roles in meetings.

PERSON

How might the following factors influence your exercise of authority in meetings?

• age

• gender

• race, ethnicity, cultural identity

• MBTI preference

• family and community background

• education and professional experience

ROLE

When you are a participant in a meeting, what influences your comfort with and confidence in exercising your formal and/or informal authority?

How often, if ever, are you a meeting facilitator?

SYSTEM

What are some of the systems in which you play a role (family, community, organizational)?

How do those systems influence the role or roles you play in meetings (family meetings, community meetings, organizational meetings)?

ROLE IN SYSTEM

What are the opportunities and challenges for you to use RBF skills in your roles in your systems?

APPLICATION:
CONSCIOUSLY ESTABLISHES ROLE IN GROUPS

You are applying this skill when:

• *you comfortably name your role in meetings.*

• *you understand the differences in your various roles.*

Being able to hold a role consciously, consistently and to convey to others clearly what role you are holding is critical to mastering the hold roles competency. Consciously establishing your role in groups is challenging and complex. During the course of a meeting or a series of conversations, you might play more than one role.

For example, if during a meeting you are the neutral facilitator and, without announcing a role change, you begin to participate in the conversation, this will create confusion about your task, role and authority in the group. Developing the skills of consciously establishing your role in a group would enable you to announce when you are stepping out of your neutral role, express your point of view as a participant, then step back into the neutral role.

Use the following five steps to make informed, conscious choices as to what role you will play and how you will play it.

1. **Compare** the different roles you and others play in meetings or conversations.

2. **Reflect** on how the boundaries of authority, role, and task vary by role.

3. **Choose** the role you hold.

4. **Consider** how to hold a role clearly and consistently.

5. **Communicate** when you change roles.

PRACTICE: ROLE CLARITY

- What is your primary role in relation to the person(s) with whom you are interacting?

- What is the work to be done and who authorized your participation?

- Given the work and the authorization, what is the role from which you can make the greatest contribution?

- Are there competing roles for you? How can you prioritize which role to play?

- How will others perceive your role? What do you need to do make your role clear?

- What is your latitude to self-authorize around a task?

- Do you need to negotiate with another person(s) to hold a particular role?

- What will you need to do to hold the role consistently and clearly?

 MASTERY:
USES AWARENESS OF B/ART TO CONTRIBUTE TO MEETING RESULTS AND MOVE FROM TALK TO ACTION

You are demonstrating mastery of this skill when:

- *you consciously make choices to hold your stated role during a meeting.*

- *you use an understanding of to align your actions with others to achieve results.*

Attached to one's roles, or assumed by people because of their roles, are the individual's and the group's perceptions of how much and what kind of authority a person has within the group and in their roles when they are not in the meeting. For purposes of RBF, the B/ART perspective is applied to bring clarity to the task that the group can choose to do. The choice is informed by the realities and possibilities of the combined B/ART of the group members within the meeting. The facilitator or the participant or the meeting convener uses B/ART to better see the system of people and the relationships in the group.[3]

Example: Using B/ART to Align Meeting Results

The following is an example of a meeting convened to design a new hire orientation session. It illuminates how a participant can use B/ART to align meeting results and seek opportunities within B/ART to move to action.

THE SITUATION

You are a line manager attending the meeting at the invitation of one of your unit supervisors, a subordinate. You delegated the task of workshop design to the supervisor. Other participants are workers and supervisors from units with new hires.

During the meeting, one of the supervisors says that some of the new hires lack the qualifications to do the work. The meeting is about to devolve into a complaint session about the hiring process.

MOVING TO ACTION WITHIN B/ART

As a participant, when recognized to speak by the facilitator or convener, you observe to the group that those who make decisions about hiring are not at the meeting (i.e., that work is not within the collective group's B/ART). You further observe that the group could decide to provide information to the Human Resources Department about the minimum qualification necessary for new hires.

Conscious of your role as a participant and using your awareness of B/ART, you offer to make note of the issues about hiring raised by the group and, *with the group's approval,* share those issues at your regularly scheduled meeting with Human Resources next week. The group accepts your offer. With this commitment from you, the group turns to its primary task — designing an orientation for new staff.

B/ART ANALYSIS

Understanding B/ART allowed you, as a participant, to contribute to the group's movement to action.

Boundary of Authority: You lacked the authority to change who would attend the meeting or the purpose of the meeting. In your participant role, you did have the authority to leverage your access to information or people who can address issues raised at the meeting.

Boundary of Role: Your role as a participant is defined by this specific meeting, one convened by one of your subordinates, whom you authorized to lead the project to design a new-hire orientation.

Boundary of Task: Your tasks included participating in the meeting, having conversations, suggesting actions, and coming to agreement about steps that lead to action, e.g., sharing the information from this meeting with the Human Resources department. In your participant role, you consciously sought approval from the group to take action — making it clear that you were not in that setting using your B/ART as a line manager. You recognized that as a participant you did not have the authority to take an issue to the Human Resources director for the group without the agreement of the group.

PRACTICE: CONSCIOUS EXERCISE OF B/ART IN ROLE

The following exercise provides guidance on how to practice consciously holding roles in meetings. As you practice holding your role, your observations of the impact of how you are holding your role on the others in the meeting will give you insights into how best to hold your role to achieve meeting results.

Lack of role clarity and consistency creates confusion in problem solving, decision making, commitments to action, and accountability. As you work toward mastering the skill of consciously establishing your role in groups, you will begin to experience the benefits of role clarity.

1. Identify two upcoming meetings where you will hold different roles.

2. Referring to the Role Analysis Matrix on page 45, specifically name the difference in B/ART for each meeting. Make notes to yourself about how you will consciously hold B/ART in each meeting. For example, if in one meeting as team leader you typically sit at the head of the table, and you are attending a meeting in the same room as a participant, you might consciously sit in a different chair and encourage the meeting convener to sit at the head of the table.

3. Practice consciously holding B/ART in role at the two meetings.

4. After the meetings, assess the experience and notice the impact on you and others of your consciously choosing and holding B/ART.

DEPLOYING RBF SKILLS IN
DIFFERENT ROLES

Using Role Clarity and B/ART to Deploy RBF Skills

At the mastery level, you can use RBF skills to bring colleagues into greater alignment. In the previous example, RBF skills can be used in different roles. The skills are the same, but they are deployed within different settings, each with a different B/ART. The figure shows four different roles and the B/ART associated with using RBF skills in each.

Before you can effectively deploy RBF skills, you need *role clarity,* which reveals what your work is. For example, a supervisor can use charting to document the work in a team meeting. Similarly, a meeting chair can use RBF skills to define clear meeting results for a board meeting. The table below gives examples of how RBF skills can be deployed in different roles.

DEPLOYING RBF SKILLS IN ROLE

RBF SKILLS & METHODS	MEETING PARTICIPANT	MEETING CONVENER	NEUTRAL RESULTS BASED FACILITATOR	TRAINER	CONSULTANT	SUPERVISOR	MEETING CHAIR
Defines Meeting Results	Can provide input to meeting results consistent with role in the meeting	Sets meeting results	Meeting results set by participants and may be changed during the meeting by the participants	Sets meeting results	Sets meeting results and/or is guided by client meeting results	Sets meeting results	Sets meeting results; may solicit recommendations from board members
Holds neutral	Is not neutral; articulates one's point of view and interest	Is not neutral; determines content and process of meeting	Neutral stance is critical; gives work back to the group	Is not neutral; conveys information	Is not neutral; conveys expert advice	Is not neutral; articulates tasks, makes decisions	Is not neutral; has final decision-making authority
Listens for	Opportunities to contribute	The agenda to be completed	Participants' responses and how they connect to the meeting result	What the participants have learned	Client needs and areas where expertise can be helpful	Progress on work and areas where decisions need to be made	Committee chairs and members' recommendations
Charts	May volunteer to chart	May be used if convener finds it useful	Is *always* done to track discussions, document decisions and commitments	May be used to support learning	May be done at the consultant or client's discretion	May be used if supervisor finds it useful	May be used if chair finds it useful

Consider the roles you typically hold in meetings. Compare the use of RBF skills in your typical roles to that of the neutral results based facilitator role from the table on page 50.

• How similar or different are these roles in the use of RBF skills?

• What might you need to do to effectively deploy RBF skills in the different roles?

PARTICIPANT PRACTICE GUIDE 1.1:
USE B/ART TO DEFINE AND DIFFERENTIATE ROLES

The guide below gives examples of how to practice the skill of using an understanding of B/ART to differentiate roles in your daily work. First, try using the skills at the awareness level in situations where there is no risk that using the skill might cause unintended or negative consequences. Once you are comfortable and confident with the more low-risk use of the skills at the awareness level, move to the application level of the skills in situations that are comparatively fault-tolerant and there is only a low to medium risk of negative consequences. Defer the use of mastery-level skills until you gain greater confidence in your use of the skill, since there may be higher risk of unanticipated consequences.

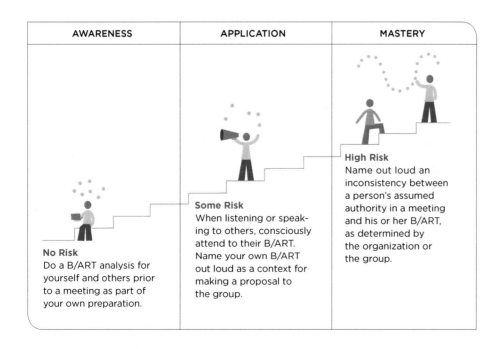

AWARENESS	APPLICATION	MASTERY
No Risk Do a B/ART analysis for yourself and others prior to a meeting as part of your own preparation.	**Some Risk** When listening or speaking to others, consciously attend to their B/ART. Name your own B/ART out loud as a context for making a proposal to the group.	**High Risk** Name out loud an inconsistency between a person's assumed authority in a meeting and his or her B/ART, as determined by the organization or the group.

SKILL 1.2: USE B/ART TO UNDERSTAND GROUP DYNAMICS AND ACHIEVE MEETING RESULTS

The B/ART lens enables you to understand group dynamics from a Person-Role-System and role-in-system perspective. The following table defines the skill and provides questions to help assess your current skill level.

AWARENESS	APPLICATION	MASTERY
Applies the concept of B/ART to understand group dynamics • *Do I use the Person-Role-System framework to assess the B/ART of meeting participants and consider how their B/ART will affect their participation?*	Applies B/ART insights to assist groups in identifying and achieving meeting results • *Do I clarify or help the group clarify the alignment of meeting results with the B/ART of the participants?* • *Do I model awareness of B/ART in meetings?*	Accurately identifies B/ART issues and brings these issues to the group's awareness • *Do I see how B/ART is affecting the group's work and then use labeling, inquiry, or hypotheses to illuminate the issues for the group?* • *Do I map who in the group holds the B/ART to address issues, make decisions, and move to action?*
→	→	→

AWARENESS:

APPLIES THE CONCEPT OF B/ART TO UNDERSTAND GROUP DYNAMICS

You are aware of this skill when:

• *you use the Person-Role-System framework to assess the B/ART of meeting participants and consider how their B/ART will affect their participation.*

In preparing for meetings, you can use information to understand potential group dynamics from a person-in-role perspective. Factors such as age, gender, professional expertise, or experience influence how a person will hold a role. The first step in applying B/ART to group dynamics is to be able to generate person-in-role hypotheses. The second step is to be able to build on that understanding and generate hypotheses about how role-in-system affects participation in meetings.

The Person-Role-System framework, which supports both person-in-role and role-in-system hypotheses, enables you to use B/ART analyses to explore how participants might engage in conversations, relate to other meeting participants, and hold authority in role in meetings. To illustrate the skill of using B/ART to

THERE IS NO HOPE OF CREATING A BETTER WORLD WITHOUT A DEEPER SCIENTIFIC INSIGHT INTO THE FUNCTION OF LEADERSHIP AND CULTURE, AND OF OTHER ESSENTIALS OF GROUP LIFE.

— KURT LEWIN

understand meeting dynamics, the following example uses MBTI preferences to generate person-in-role hypotheses about how people hold their decision-making authority in their role.

Step One: Person-in-Role Hypotheses

Consciously generating hypotheses is an application of Lewin's principles of action research or action learning to better understand group dynamics.[4] The figure adapted from Peddler's *Power of Action Learning,*[5] illustrates the role of hypotheses in the action learning cycle.

In the Person-Role-System framework, a person's MBTI preference is one factor that can inform how he or she holds decision-making authority in role. For example, an SF supervisor might make decisions based on people's needs, and an ST supervisor might make decisions based on enforcing standard practices. Awareness of MBTI preferences about decision making can inform the hypotheses generated about people's behavior in meetings and how they might exercise their decision-making authority in role.

The table below describes SF, NF, ST, and NT preferences regarding the information used (input bias) and shared (output bias) when making decisions, and the basis for decisions (operational bias).[6] To better understand how MBTI can inform person-in-role hypotheses, use the information in the table to generate hypotheses about how two different supervisors — one, an SF, and the other, an ST — might approach a decision about how to handle an employee who persistently arrives late to work. Generate hypotheses about what information each might gather and how each might approach the decision.

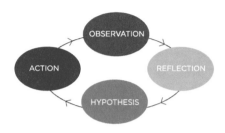

ADAPTATION OF PEDDLER'S POWER OF ACTION LEARNING

DIFFERENTIAL IMPACT: MBTI AND DECISION MAKING

PAIR	INPUT BIAS Information sought and used	OUTPUT BIAS Basis for generating alternatives	OPERATIONAL BIAS Basis for decisions
SF	The opinions of specific people (may ignore hard data)	Options supported by important people	What people in their situation want and need
NF	Symbols, imagery, and metaphors (may ignore practical data)	Analogies and novel ideas	Associations from similar experiences or vision of the future
ST	Specific facts (may ignore patterns)	Problem-solving models that have worked in the past	Regularity, structure, and fit with standard practices
NT	Systematic (may ignore specifics that differ from model)	Data that confirm conceptual pattern	Logical categorization based on their conceptual pattern

The following practice will strengthen your ability to use MBTI preferences to generate person-in-role hypotheses about people's behaviors in meetings.

> Reflect on the hypotheses that you generated about the SF and ST supervisors from the table on page 53.
>
> • What insights do you have about how MBTI preference might influence people's behavior in meetings when people are working to make a decision together?
>
> Reflect on these insights. The next time you convene or attend a decision-making meeting, generate multiple hypotheses about your own participation and the participation of others based on MBTI insights.

Step Two: Role-in-System Hypotheses

Role-in-system is the perspective that enables you to see how systems that authorize or define a role shape people's behavior in role. For example, the supervisor of caseworkers in a clinical setting may supervise five to seven people and provide in-depth supervision to ensure that the appropriate decisions are made in difficult cases. In contrast, the supervisor in a manufacturing plant might manage many more workers doing routine tasks and not provide individual supervision of those tasks. In each instance, the supervisor has the B/ART to oversee the quality of performance; however, the role-in-system perspective illuminates how the roles differ in execution. Information can be gathered about role-in-system from many different sources. Organizational charts can show how the systems define authority and accountability. Titles can signal both function and level of authority.

PRACTICE: USING THE B/ART LENS TO GENERATE HYPOTHESES

In the exercise on the following page, you have an opportunity to use role-in-system information as well as person-in-role information to generate hypotheses about behavior in meetings.

The exercise includes an organizational chart showing the positions of all the people in the meeting and their relationship to each other and a table showing the composition analysis of two group members.

Meeting Purpose

A problem-solving meeting to develop solutions to a cross-departmental information technology challenge.

Participants

The Chief of Operations, who reports to the President and supervises all the service delivery departments — see organization chart below — convenes the meeting. Participants include the directors of the service departments, the director of the Information Technology (IT) department, and the manager of the IT Help Desk Unit, who reports to the IT director. The IT director does not report to the Chief of Operations but directly to the Chief of Support Services, a peer of the Chief of Operations.

Meeting Design and Results

The meeting design calls for all participants to work as peers while making decisions about how to address the IT challenge in all its dimensions — hardware, software, development and use of technology, and training and user support. The meeting results will be a set of recommendations that the Chief of Operations will make to the President after it is reviewed by the Chief of Support Services.

B/ART and Person-Role-System Information

The organizational chart and the Person-Role-System information in the table below provide information about the director of IT and the manager of the help desk unit. Now, take the time to study the information from the different sources, imagine the scenario, and then generate your hypotheses.

SCENARIO ORGANIZATION CHART

PERSON-ROLE-SYSTEM COMPOSITION ANALYSIS

TITLE	DIRECTOR, IT DEPARTMENT	MANAGER, IT HELP DESK UNIT
Gender	Male	Female
MBTI decision-making preference	SF Finalizes decisions by exploring feelings and the impact of decisions on people	NT Finalizes decisions by applying external criteria
Tenure with the IT Department	4 years	7 years
Education	Master's in Business Administration	Master's in Computer Science
Familiarity with the issues	Very familiar with the end-user frustrations	Very familiar with the technical features
Orientation toward the meeting results	Concerned that additional user interface requirements will strain an already over-burdened budget	Wants the Chief of Operations to require that all staff in service units receive IT training to reduce calls to the help desk
	Is currently in the midst of a 3-year process to upgrade business systems; the project is missing deadlines and is over budget	Knows from user calls that a number of the business systems need software upgrades and that hardware in many parts of the organization is substandard

Use the following questions to generate multiple hypotheses about each person who might participate in the meeting:

Authority
• What might be the source of their authority? e.g., from their formal authority? from expertise? from other sources? How might that affect their participation?

Characteristics
• How might other factors (MBTI? gender? seniority? orientation to the results?) affect their participation in decision making?

Relationships
• How might their relationship with each other, the convener, and the other participants affect their participation in the meeting?

After you generate your own hypotheses, compare them to the possible hypotheses in the following table.

POSSIBLE HYPOTHESES FOR PARTICIPANT BEHAVIOR

AREA OF ANALYSIS	DIRECTOR, IT DEPARTMENT	MANAGER, IT HELP DESK UNIT
MBTI **(person in role)**	1. Might be very interested in meeting end-user needs and very focused on making the directors of the service units feel good about the solution 2. Might be worried about the help desk manager feeling burned out and be supportive of the manager's interests even in the face of budget constraints	1. Might be frustrated that end users are not using the approved criteria for accessing the help desk and unsympathetic to users who do not read the manuals before calling 2. Might be applying criteria of end-user satisfaction to advocate a more rapid completion of business systems and increased levels of support during transition from old to new systems
Authority **(role in system)**	1. Might hesitate to use formal authority because background is in business not technology 2. Might exert formal authority to block commitments of resources due to budget constraints	1. Might exert authority from expertise (IT) and formal role (detailed information about user behavior from help desk) to advance agenda about training for end users 2. Might use informal authority of longer tenure to subtly challenge supervisor, the IT director, to make an ally of the Chief of Operations and build support for budget increases
Relationships	1. Might be very cautious in the meeting because the Chief of Operations is a peer to his supervisor, the Chief of Support Services 2. Might be protective of the help desk manager, to preserve their good working relationship	1. Might be deferential to supervisor while in a meeting to show loyalty with their shared customers — the service delivery units 2. Might challenge her supervisor, the IT director, because she feels he is an ally of the end users and not supportive of enforcing the criteria for accessing the help desk

PRACTICE: GENERATING B/ART HYPOTHESES DURING MEETINGS

Reflect on the multiple hypotheses that you generated in the exercise above.

• What insights do you have about using the lenses of MBTI, Person-Role-System, and B/ART to generate hypotheses about people's behavior in meetings, specifically during decision making?

Reflect on these insights. The next time you convene or attend a decision-making meeting, generate multiple hypotheses about your own participation and the participation of others in the meeting.

Reflect on your own and others' participation after the meeting. How did your and others' participation compare to your hypotheses?

APPLICATION:
APPLIES B/ART INSIGHTS TO ASSIST GROUPS IN IDENTIFYING
AND ACHIEVING MEETING RESULTS

You are applying this skill when:

• *you clarify or help the group clarify the alignment of meeting results with the B/ART of the participants.*

• *you model awareness of B/ART in meetings.*

In exploring the B/ART of a group, the most useful question often is: *What is the work that the people in this room can do together?*

For example, the school superintendent operates within the educational system and holds authority delegated by the board of education. The superintendent's authority and role differ from a school principal within that same educational system.

When the people at the meeting understand their collective boundaries of authority and roles, they can focus on who can do what within their respective systems. This focus illuminates the tasks that the members of the group can accomplish during, as well as outside of, the meeting. Meeting participants' roles in meetings are informed by the roles they play outside the meetings.

The following scenario provides an example of how clarity about B/ART can be used by participants to have an effective meeting.

Example: Using B/ART to Clarify Meeting Results

In this scenario, a group of frontline workers are gathered together to implement a new process. The workers in the meeting are spending a lot of time complaining about their supervisors and wishing that their supervisors had made a different decision.

However, the decision to implement the new process is not within the role or authority of these frontline workers. After some complaining, however, the frontline workers realize that it is within their role and authority to develop recommendations to their supervisors about the best way to implement the new process.

Within their B/ART, the group discusses the content and phrasing of the recommendation, the person and method for delivering the recommendation, and who can have informal conversations with people to develop support for the recommendations. At the end of the meeting, the workers have developed a recommendation for their supervisors and committed to the next steps to deliver that recommendation and maximize the possibility that it will be adopted. In this scenario, by developing a recommendation, the frontline workers have used clarity about their B/ART to align the boundaries of authority and role to accomplish a task.

Consider meetings that you attend and assess how clear you and others are about your B/ART and theirs. Then reflect on the following:

• What might I do in an upcoming meeting to take actions aligned with my B/ART?

• How might I clarify the collective B/ART of all those in the meeting?

MASTERY:
ACCURATELY IDENTIFIES B/ART ISSUES AND BRINGS THESE ISSUES TO THE GROUP'S AWARENESS

You are demonstrating mastery of this skill when:

• *you see how B/ART affects the group's work and then use labeling, inquiry or hypotheses to illuminate the issues for the group.*

• *you map who in the group holds the B/ART to address issues, make decisions, and move to action.*

Examples: Identifying B/ART Issues

B/ART issues arise in many situations. They can occur when a member of the group is behaving as if he or she has authority over a peer, or when two or more members of the group are in conflict about the group's scope of work and are asserting their point of view based on different sources of authority (e.g., one might reference the authority of expertise and the other might reference the authority of seniority of experience). A group member may use informal authority to prevent a conversation that would make the person feel vulnerable. A group member may challenge the authority of the convener by resisting requests to focus on the meeting's purpose and, instead, bring up unrelated issues.

Often many people in the meeting see or feel these dynamics but do not know how to label them or feel comfortable in bringing them up to the group. Mastery of the skill entails being aware of the group dynamics as they occur and bringing the issues to the group's attention. Developing mastery occurs when you can name and share out loud observations about B/ART issues.

• What emotions, worries about consequences, or discomfort prevent me from raising B/ART issues?

• How might I get comfortable with raising B/ART issues?

This exercise is based on Peter Senge's[7] Left Hand Column/Right Hand Column approach to raising the unconscious assumptions that guide people's participation in conversations.

During a meeting when people seem to be stuck and unable to move to action, take a piece of paper and draw three vertical lines. Label the columns as follows:

Right Column: What people are doing or saying out loud that is contributing to the group being stuck.

Left Column: What are some B/ART hypotheses about what people are thinking or feeling but not saying out loud.

Far Left Column: How would you label what you are hearing and seeing, and what might you do within your B/ART to bring this to the awareness of the group?

The exercise enables you to pay attention to what is not being said as well as what is being said. As you perform this exercise, pay attention to what is undiscussed or undiscussable about B/ART issues that may be a barrier that prevents the group from moving from talk to action. Start on the right with your observation and move to the left to generate hypotheses and labels.

WORK FROM RIGHT TO LEFT

FAR LEFT COLUMN	LEFT COLUMN	RIGHT COLUMN
What is a label for what I am seeing and hearing? **What can I do with what I know within my B/ART to help the group move forward?**	**What are some B/ART hypotheses about what people are thinking or feeling but not saying out loud?**	**What is being said and by whom that is contributing to the group being stuck?** **What is not being said?**
Example label **Label:** Overuse of hierarchical authority, quenching engagement. **Action in Role** As a participant, you can bring the potential B/ART issue to the group's awareness by acknowledging the exercise of authority and reframing the work within that hierarchical context. **Statement** *Ms./Mr. Supervisor, you are sharing your thinking about the solutions. What would be most helpful to you — some feedback on those solutions or some additional ideas?*	**Example multiple hypotheses** **Hypothesis #1:** The supervisor does not trust the meeting participants' competence and is de-authorizing them so they no longer have the B/ART of contributing to solutions. *(What the supervisor is not saying is that he or she doesn't trust the subordinates.)* **Hypothesis #2:** The supervisor already knows the solution his or her manager wants implemented and is only pretending to authorize the problem solving of the participants. The supervisor is not holding his or her own B/ART of bringing input to his or her manager's solutions. *(What the supervisor is not saying is that he or she is unwilling to challenge the boss.)*	**Example observation** The supervisor who has convened the problem-solving meeting is asking for input from the participants. However, instead of waiting for responses, the supervisor fills every silence with his or her own ideas and cuts others off when they try to express their ideas. The meeting is stuck because the group is neither generating nor discussing ideas. The meeting participants by their body language and silence are **not** saying what they feel. You observe sidelong glances and people looking down at the table rather than at the supervisor. *(What the participants are not saying is that they believe the supervisor will not listen to them.)*

The guide below outlines practices that you can bring to your daily work to strengthen your capacity to use B/ART as a lens for understanding group dynamics.

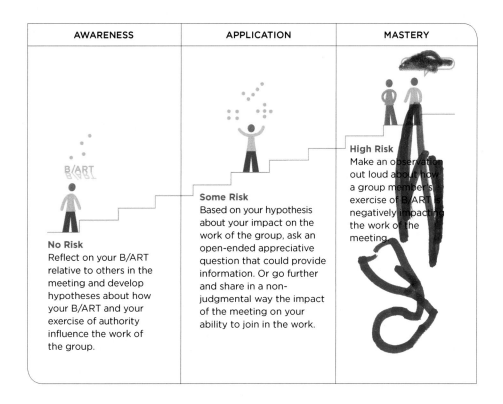

AWARENESS	APPLICATION	MASTERY
No Risk Reflect on your B/ART relative to others in the meeting and develop hypotheses about how your B/ART and your exercise of authority influence the work of the group.	**Some Risk** Based on your hypothesis about your impact on the work of the group, ask an open-ended appreciative question that could provide information. Or go further and share in a non-judgmental way the impact of the meeting on your ability to join in the work.	**High Risk** Make an observation out loud about how a group member's exercise of B/ART is negatively impacting the work of the meeting.

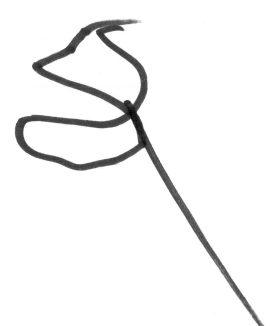

SKILL 1.3: HOLD NEUTRAL FACILITATOR ROLE

A critical element of the RBF method is that groups own and act on decisions. To ensure that the decision-making authority is exercised by the group and not inappropriately held by a facilitator, RBF has a specific skill that defines how the facilitator role is held in meetings. The table below defines the skill and provides questions you can use to determine your level of mastery in holding this role.

AWARENESS	APPLICATION	MASTERY
Knows the role of neutral facilitator and is aware of what it takes not to seek one's own personal agenda • *Do I employ specific practices to maintain the neutral facilitator role and not use the authority of the facilitator to pursue my own agenda?*	Holds the neutral role most of the time • *Do I refrain from using my expertise or authority to influence group decisions?* • *Do I recognize when I am not holding the neutral facilitator role?*	Consistently holds the neutral role • *Do I have a repertoire of practices to acknowledge lapses and return to neutral?*

The Importance of Neutral Facilitators

The role of the neutral facilitator is central to RBF tools and methods. Holding a neutral role requires the facilitator to give the work back to the group and not use his or her authority to pursue a personal agenda. The neutral facilitator role makes it possible for the group members to answer their own questions and make their own decisions.

The neutral facilitator role can be held by one person for the duration of the meeting — either a member of the group authorized to hold that role or someone who is an outside facilitator. In either instance, holding neutral in an explicit facilitator role occurs when the group authorizes the person to perform specific tasks in support of the group achieving its articulated purpose and within its commonly understood boundaries of time and place.

The agreement regarding the role of the facilitator can be established prior to the meeting, in discussion with the meeting's conveners; at the beginning of the meeting, when the facilitator explicitly asks the group members what they do and don't want from the facilitator; or during the meeting, when either a meeting convener or a participant is authorized by the group to take up the neutral role.

AND THE PEOPLE WILL SAY, WE DID IT OURSELVES

— LAO TSU

The neutral role requires that the group answer its own questions and prohibits the person holding the neutral role from answering the question for the group. However, that neutrality — i.e., ensuring that whatever answer the group comes up with is their answer — does not extend to a neutrality about meeting results or meeting processes. The neutral facilitator has the task and authority to support the group in achieving meeting results.

In RBF, the concept of B/ART is used to determine whether it is appropriate and/or feasible for a meeting participant or meeting convener to hold the neutral role. Developing the competency to hold the neutral role and knowing when and how to play that role can be both challenging and rewarding.

Groups *want* neutral facilitators. In hundreds of facilitation workshops, when participants are asked to describe the characteristics of an effective facilitator, they always describe their desire for a facilitator to play a neutral role. Their preferences are shown below.

WHAT GROUPS WANT AND DON'T WANT FROM A FACILITATOR

GROUPS ALMOST ALWAYS WANT	GROUPS SOMETIMES WANT	GROUPS NEVER WANT
Focus on task within time	Relationship building	A facilitator with his or her own agenda
Movement	Synthesis	
Inclusive participation	Observations	

AWARENESS:
KNOWS THE ROLE OF NEUTRAL FACILITATOR AND IS AWARE OF WHAT IT TAKES NOT TO SEEK OWN PERSONAL AGENDA

You are aware of this skill when:

• *you refrain from using your expertise or authority to influence group decisions.*

• *you recognize when you are not holding the neutral facilitator role.*

B/ART for the Neutral Facilitator

The role of neutral facilitator takes place within the specific boundaries of author-ity, role, and task. Bion's work on groups highlighted the importance of the facilitator being able to hold steady in his or her role while simultaneously experi-encing and reflecting on the experience of what is occurring in group.[8] The table on the following page describes the B/ART of the neutral facilitator.

THE TRICK IS TO BE ABLE TO THINK UNDER FIRE, TO KEEP SOME PART OF YOUR MIND ABLE TO REFLECT ON EXPERIENCE WHILE HAVING THE EXPERIENCE.

— ROBERT M. YOUNG

- Have you ever been in a meeting that felt as though the facilitator had a personal agenda?

- What was your reaction?

- What was the reaction of the group?

FACILITATOR'S B/ART

B/ART ELEMENT	Definition of Element	Application to Neutral Facilitator Role
RBF BOUNDARY	time, territory	Set for a meeting, segment of a meeting, series of meetings, or any formal or informal interactions of people convened or gathered for a purpose
AUTHORITY	the right to do work	Given by the group to the facilitator (e.g., the group authorizes the role of the facilitator to support the group in accomplishing meeting results)
ROLE	the function of the person	Giving the work back to the group in a way that the group can do its work within the RBF framework, framing questions, synthesizing the group's answers, offering mental models for the group to use, and remaining neutral (not inserting personal answers)
TASK	the work of the group	Listening and speaking around a series of tasks (e.g., facilitating conversations that collectively enable the group to own its action, producing results outside the meeting) — a relational and analytic function

Holding Neutral: What Is Your Practice?

Holding a neutral role is not only challenging but is also sometimes not appropriate. Being aware of how you are not neutral in other roles can help you in holding the neutral role when necessary. This awareness will also help you notice that when you feel challenged to hold the neutral role, it may be because consciously or unconsciously you are drawn to another role, e.g., the role of consultant with the authority of expertise or the role of supervisor with the ability to tell people what to do.

- Where are you most challenged to hold neutral?

- When is it appropriate for you to hold neutral?

- What is a practice you can adopt to hold the neutral role?

PRACTICE: HOLDING NEUTRAL IN A VARIETY OF SETTINGS

Examine the examples below of how to hold neutral. Consider how difficult the described method would be for you in a variety of roles, situations, and settings

HOLDING NEUTRAL ENTAILS	SITUATIONS SETTINGS WHERE METHOD WOULD BE DIFFICULT
Setting aside one's own interests in the outcome of a conversation or meeting	
Creating space for people to speak without regard to personal preference or other factors that can skew participation	
Giving the work of problem solving and decision making back to the group	
Not expressing agreement or disagreement with your favored or disfavored point of view verbally or nonverbally	
Being appreciative to points of view that you disagree with	
Using a focus on meeting results to enable the group to make choices about the content and sequence of their work	
Declaring when you are no longer able to hold neutral	

APPLICATION:

HOLDS THE NEUTRAL ROLE MOST OF THE TIME

You are applying this skill when:

- *you refrain from using expertise or authority to influence group decisions.*
- *you recognize when you are not holding the neutral facilitator role.*

Steps to Holding the Role of Neutral Facilitator

1. Establish your role by asking effective questions:

- What do you want from this facilitation?
- As your facilitator, I will ... Is that okay?
- Is there anything else that I can do to help?

2. Use a variety of approaches to remain in your neutral role (role discipline):

- Develop awareness of your own reactions to the role and practice becoming comfortable with the role. For example, use a book like *Comfortable with Uncertainty* by Chodron[9] as a meditation guide.
- Develop greater awareness of what topics, issues, or behaviors trigger a strong reaction in you. Practice pausing, breathing, internally acknowledging your reaction, and mentally setting your reaction aside to remain neutral.

Am I holding a neutral role?

Will I be more effective listening rather than speaking?

How do I facilitate the conversation to encourage others to turn comments, ideas, etc., into proposals?

Am I within the boundary of my authority? My role? My task?

PRACTICE: HOW WILL YOU HOLD NEUTRAL?

- What can you do to stay neutral and not answer the questions of the group?
- How will you know that you are no longer holding neutral?
- What might you be feeling when you are not holding neutral?
- What might you see or hear in the group that will signal that you are not holding neutral?

MASTERY:
CONSISTENTLY HOLDS THE NEUTRAL ROLE

You are demonstrating mastery of this skill when:

• *you use a repertoire of practices to acknowledge lapses and return to neutral.*

When the neutral role is held at a high level of mastery, the group knows its own work and members can do it together. Therefore, a key skill in holding the role is to have a repertoire of methods to give the work back to the group.

Repertoire of Methods for Holding the Neutral Role

At the beginning of the meeting: *Establish your role by receiving the authority of the group to facilitate.*

• Clarify your role from the start.

• Help the group members work together to identify their desired results and develop their agenda.

• Affirm meeting results with the group.

• Affirm or obtain the group's authorization for your role and tasks.

• Use a check-in that establishes the group's ownership of meeting results and the group members' relationships to each other.

During the meeting: *Give the work back to the group.*

• Be aware of your own actions and reactions and observe their impact on the group.

• Notice when you think you have the right answer or have a desire to advocate for a point of view and check yourself to ensure you are neutral about content.

• Be aware of when you are dominating the discussion or working too hard and use silence, synthesis, or an Effective Question to give the work back to the group.

• Hold your role from the balcony[10] and label what is occurring in the group or ask the group to name what is happening.

• Summarize the work and ask the group members what they want to do.

• When a group member asks you what to do or for an answer, acknowledge the request and invite the group to propose a course of action or an answer.

• Invite reflection, paired conversations, and small-group conversations as ways for the group to develop options of what to do and how to do it.

• In the rare instance you step out of neutral, name what you are doing and return to neutral as quickly as possible.

- Make the group aware of the lack of alignment with meeting results and/or their own decisions. Then ask the group what they want to do — either return to the original meeting results or decisions or adopt new ones.

At the end of the meeting: *Review action and next steps.*

- Review decisions and commitments to action (e.g., who will do what when).

- Use a check-out that illuminates whether people got their meeting results and how they feel about each other and/or the meeting experience.

 PARTICIPANT PRACTICE GUIDE 1.3:
HOLD NEUTRAL FACILITATOR ROLE

Holding the neutral role is a challenge when you are passionate about an issue or deeply invested in a point of view. However, sometimes there are opportunities for practicing holding neutral that can benefit you and the group. Below are examples of how to hold neutral in the participant role.

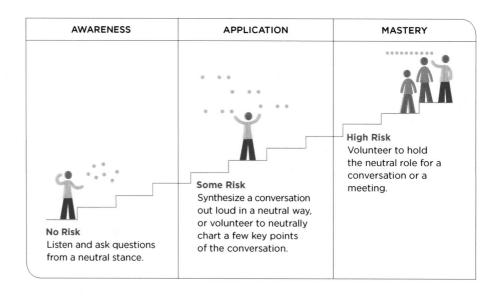

AWARENESS	APPLICATION	MASTERY
No Risk Listen and ask questions from a neutral stance.	**Some Risk** Synthesize a conversation out loud in a neutral way, or volunteer to neutrally chart a few key points of the conversation.	**High Risk** Volunteer to hold the neutral role for a conversation or a meeting.

SKILL 1.4: GIVE THE WORK BACK TO THE GROUP

A critical element of the RBF method is that groups own and act on decisions. To ensure that the decision-making authority is exercised by the group and not inappropriately held by a facilitator, RBF has a specific skill that defines how the facilitator role is held in meetings. The table below defines the skill and provides questions you can use to determine your level of mastery in holding this role.

AWARENESS	APPLICATION	MASTERY
Understands the role of the facilitator in giving the work back to the group • *Do I refer questions about the work back to the group?* • *Do I patiently hold the neutral facilitator role while the group takes time to find its own solutions and make its own decisions?*	Applies a repertoire of methods to give the work back to the group • *Do I recognize pivotal moments when to give the work back to the group?* • *Do I go to the balcony to invite group awareness and insights for forward movement?*	Consistently gives the work back to the group • *Do I use observation, inquiry, and reflective practice to invite the group to move forward?* • *Do I use humor, physical activity, intuition, spiritual awareness, and analytical insights to illuminate the group's capacity to do its hardest work?*
→	→	→

AWARENESS:

UNDERSTANDS THE ROLE OF THE FACILITATOR IN GIVING THE WORK BACK TO THE GROUP

You are aware of this skill when:

- *you refer questions about the work back to the group.*

- *you patiently hold the neutral facilitator role while the group takes time to find its own solutions and make its own decisions.*

Giving the work back to the group is an essential skill in maintaining the neutral facilitator role. The group must answer its own questions and not look to the facilitator to answer them for the group. The Acknowledge, Rephrase, Explore (ARE) technique is a core method to give the work back to the group.[11]

ARE – A method to give work back to the group

Acknowledge: Body language conveys listening.

• Lean forward.

• Offer a little listening noise.

• Demonstrate attention through nonverbal cues.

Rephrase: Empathetic responses address feelings.

• Use your own words to reflect your understanding.

• Validate that what was heard is what was said.

Explore: Ask open-ended questions to members of the group to gain deeper understanding and to help them address their own issues.

PRACTICE: GIVING BACK TO THE GROUP – ARE

The following exercise is designed to give you practice using ARE, even in the face of strong opinions or emotions. Using ARE in a practice setting helps you use it during meetings to give work back to the group.

> With a learning partner, i.e., someone who will work with you to develop skill, use the following five steps to practice ARE. The exercise usually takes about 20 minutes from beginning to end.
>
> 1. Review the elements of ARE and the SBI method of feedback.
>
> 2. Choose a hot-button topic on which the two of you disagree and have strong feelings about.
>
>   • A hot-button topic is one that evokes strong emotions in both the speaker and the listener. Hot-button topics often reflect people's values or beliefs about controversial issues.
>
>   • You will each have a chance to facilitate the conversation by using ARE while listening to your learning partner talk about the topic. Decide who will be the facilitator first.
>
> 3. The first facilitator uses ARE while his or her learning partner talks about the topic for five minutes.
>
> 4. After 5 minutes, the facilitator self-assesses his or her use of ARE and ability to remain neutral and give the work back to the learning partner, and the learning partner offers feedback using the SBI approach.
>
> 5. The learning partner now becomes the facilitator and repeats steps 3 and 4 on the same topic.

Reflect on this experience and explore insights about holding the neutral role by answering these questions.

• What insights do I have about the challenge of holding neutral?

• What are my hot-button topics? Personally? Professionally?

• What was the impact on me and on my partner of using ARE?

• What do I need to practice in order to hold neutral as a facilitator?

APPLICATION:

APPLIES A REPERTOIRE OF METHODS TO GIVE THE WORK BACK TO THE GROUP

You are applying this skill when:

• *you recognize pivotal moments when you should give the work back to the group.*

• *you go to the balcony to invite group awareness and insights for forward movement.*

The next time you facilitate a meeting and notice that you are working harder than the group, e.g., talking more and/or engaging with a higher energy level than the participants, use the method of going to the balcony to notice what is happening in group. The following repertoire of methods can be used to give the work back to the group.

• When you notice that too much attention is focused on you as the facilitator, physically step back and the next time someone addresses a comment to you — gesture to the group. Use body language to signal that the group owns the conversation.

• When the group is having a hard time focusing on one conversation, point to the flip chart header to remind them of the topic.

• When the group is coming back to the same topic repetitively without resolving the issue, let the group know how many times they have discussed the issue and ask them what they would like to do to move forward.

Going to the Balcony: Another Method to Hold Neutral

Sometimes giving the work back to the group is hard because you have lost your awareness of your role and become part of the group. Heifetz has a very useful metaphor that can help you hold on to the neutral role. Imagine that the participants in the meeting are dancers on a dance floor. If you join them on the dance floor, you only see your immediate surroundings. If you go to the balcony and look down, you gain perspective.

PRACTICE: GOING TO THE BALCONY

Imagine that you are up above, on a balcony, looking down at the meeting participants and the discussion. From the balcony ask yourself the following questions:

• What is happening in the group?

• What conversations are the group having?

• What conversations are the group not having?

• What can I name to help the group see its work?

• What Effective Question can I ask that will help the group do its work?

MASTERY:
CONSISTENTLY GIVES THE WORK BACK TO THE GROUP

You are demonstrating mastery of this skill when:

• *you use reflective practice to invite those holding the capacity to move the group forward to make observations, share hypotheses, or make proposals.*

• *you use humor, physical activity, intuition, spiritual awareness, and analytical insights to illuminate the group's capacity to do its hardest work.*

The dynamics of any particular meeting can inform your choice about whether to use a skill and which skill to use. In assessing the situation, take the opportunity to silently go to the balcony, make observations to yourself, and reflect on your own hypotheses about the causes of the meeting dynamics you are observing. When you label what you see, you are giving a name to your observations, which may help the group do its work.

For example, from the balcony you might observe that every time the group is about to make a decision, one or more people will divert attention to new issues. You might label that behavior "flight from decision making." That label might help you to consider whether the flight is to avoid conflict, avoid work, and/or take the group in another direction. Based on your hypothesis, you might then share it and invite the group to weigh in with their observations and hypotheses.

Flight from decision making is one form of work avoidance. Other forms of work avoidance and what you might do to support the group in its work are highlighted below.[12]

- What common forms of work avoidance do you observe in meetings?

- What might you do or say in the meeting to name or label the work being avoided and to invite the group to pick up that work?

TIPS: HANDLING WORK AVOIDANCE

IF YOU SEE THIS	USE THIS LABEL AND TAKE THIS ACTION
People checking out, showing low energy, and being apathetic about the work	**LABEL:** Boredom — reflecting lack of cognitive engagement because people don't see the benefit to them. **ACTION:** Have people take a moment to breathe, refresh, move around, and regain physical energy. When they return, ask them what is the work that they can do that will benefit them personally. Facilitate a conversation about individual interests and make links to work that can address those interests.
People indicating that their participation doesn't matter, cynical comments about the work not being meaningful or authentic	**LABEL:** Passive aggressive — reflecting that they feel compelled to be there and resent being asked to do the work. **ACTION:** Acknowledge that many people may feel that they have to be there and would perhaps rather be somewhere else. Invite people to journal what might make the work meaningful to them. Facilitate a conversation to illuminate options.
People not trusting their own expertise and deferring to external authorities to answer the questions; circular conversations about the current situation and the impossibility of the task	**LABEL:** Failure avoidance — reflecting a sense that the task is not doable or that the people in the room are not competent or can't succeed. **ACTION:** Acknowledge the difficulty of the task. Invite people to consider what helps them approach a seemingly impossible task. Have people share their experience and insights about working on impossible tasks. Have people pair up and create a wise saying or slogan that the group can use. Use light heartedness and humor to stimulate their creative energy.
People persistently asking the facilitator to use his or her expertise to answer the questions or constantly deferring to those with hierarchical authority	**LABEL:** Learned helplessness — reflecting patterns of behavior in the group that discount initiative and inhibit proactive problem solving. **ACTION:** List all the issues that the group is struggling to address. Invite participants to consider what they know about the issues, what they don't know about the issues, and who in the group might be able to share knowledge or find knowledge to address the issues. Use that information to support the group in using what it knows and being proactive about finding out more.

PARTICIPANT PRACTICE GUIDE 1.4:
GIVE THE WORK BACK TO THE GROUP

As a participant, you will have many opportunities to use the skill of giving the work back to the group. Begin with low-risk opportunities and as your skill develops move to higher risk uses of the skill. The guide below provides methods of giving the work to the group in different settings.

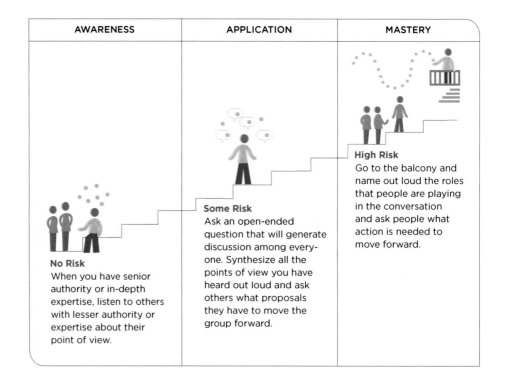

AWARENESS	APPLICATION	MASTERY

No Risk
When you have senior authority or in-depth expertise, listen to others with lesser authority or expertise about their point of view.

Some Risk
Ask an open-ended question that will generate discussion among everyone. Synthesize all the points of view you have heard out loud and ask others what proposals they have to move the group forward.

High Risk
Go to the balcony and name out loud the roles that people are playing in the conversation and ask people what action is needed to move forward.

NOTES:

[1] Green and Molenkamp. *The BART System of Group and Organizational Analysis.* 2005.

[2] White. *Person-Role-System Framework Briefing Note.* 2013.

[3] Oshry. *Seeing Systems.* Berrett-Koehler Publishers. 1996.

[4] Lewin. *Action Research and Minority Problems.* J Soc. Issues. 1946.

[5] Peddler. *The Power of Action Learning.* Gower Publishing. 4th Edition. 2012.

[6] Haler and Pini. *Blazing International Trails in Strategic Decision-Making Research.* Proceedings of the Myers-Briggs Type Indicator and Leadership. National Leadership Institute. 1994.

[7] Senge. *Fifth Discipline Fieldbook.* Crown Publishing Group. 1994.

[8] Young. *Bion and Experiences in Group.* http://human-nature.com/rmyoung/papers/pap148h.html

[9] Chodron. *Comfortable with Uncertainty.* Shambala Publications. 2004.

[10] The concept of going to the balcony is based on Heifetz's concept of adaptive leadership, as described in *Leadership Without Easy Answers.*

[11] Courtesy of Steven Jones and Victoria Goddard-Truitt.

[12] Farvis and Seifert. Work avoidance as a manifestation of hostility, helplessness, and boredom. *The Alberta Journal of Educational Research.* Vol. XLVIU, No. 2. Summer, 2002.

HOLD CONVERSATIONS

DEFINITION: LISTEN WITH OPENNESS, CURIOSITY, AND ATTENTIVENESS TO FRAME DIALOGUES THAT ACHIEVE MEETING RESULTS

LISTENING LOOKS EASY,
BUT IT'S NOT SIMPLE.
EVERY HEAD IS A WORLD.

– CUBAN PROVERB

SKILLS FOR THIS COMPETENCY

2.1 DEMONSTRATE APPRECIATIVE OPENNESS

2.2 USE CONTEXT STATEMENTS, EFFECTIVE QUESTIONS, AND LISTEN FORS

In this chapter, you'll learn the competency of holding conversations — something each of us does every day, but not necessarily in a way that leads to results. Two key skills can make conversations more effective: demonstrating appreciative openness — which involves listening and attentiveness — and using intentional statements, questions, and prompts to generate action and results.

> **Conversation:** people listening to and talking about the same thing at the same time

SKILL 2.1: DEMONSTRATE APPRECIATIVE OPENNESS

The fundamental importance of appreciative listening becomes apparent if you have ever been in a meeting in which people are not listening to each other and the facilitator is not a good listener. Frustration builds as the conversations become increasingly repetitive, as people try to be heard, or overly quiet, as people disengage. The antidote is to develop the skill of listening so that people know that they are heard and are encouraged to hear others. The table below defines the skill of appreciative openness and poses questions to assess skill level and direct practice.

AWARENESS	APPLICATION	MASTERY
Understands the primacy of listening as a skill; is aware of and monitors own listening behavior	Attends to participants to ensure all ideas and voices are heard	Consistently demonstrates interest in conversations of others throughout the meeting
• Am I genuinely curious about the conversation and what is being said?	• Am I aware of filters that may influence what is heard and not heard for myself and others?	• Do I keep my own interests and interpretations in check (be neutral) when I am listening?
• Am I aware of when I am consciously listening and when I am not?	• Do I use strategies to remain open, appreciative, and in the moment?	• Do I use a variety of strategies to engage the speaker (e.g., silence, nonverbal, EQs)?
• Do I make conscious choices about when to speak and when to listen?	• Do I use nonverbal cues of attentiveness and interest?	• Do I quickly notice lack of listening, acknowledge the lack, and self-correct?
	• Do I ask Effective Questions (EQs) to gain insight into assumptions, facts, and points of view and verify understanding of what was said?	• Do I maintain focused listening for the duration of a meeting?

AWARENESS:

UNDERSTANDS PRIMACY OF LISTENING AS A SKILL AND IS AWARE OF AND MONITORS OWN LISTENING BEHAVIOR

You are aware of this skill when:

- *you are genuinely curious about the conversation and what is being said.*

- *you are aware of when you are consciously listening and when you are not.*

- *you make conscious choices about when to speak and when to listen.*

Awareness of how you listen and practice appreciative listening is necessary to hold the neutral role. Appreciative listening also enhances your ability to communicate effectively in other roles. Use the following Appreciative Listening Checklist[1] to establish your baseline for practice.

Appreciative Listening Checklist #1

Consider to what extent you display these characteristics when you are in conversations. Also, consider how your listening might change depending on your role — as a participant, a facilitator, or a meeting chair.

- Being quiet while the other person is talking

- Being attentive to the speaker by not performing other tasks

- Looking at the person who is speaking

- Being aware of tone, facial expressions, and words

- Thinking about what the speaker is saying rather than thinking about what you want to say next

Are there other ways that you display appreciative listening? As you consider your own current practice of appreciative listening, consider how persistently and how frequently you are in that state of appreciative listening. Most people without intention and attention are only intermittently fully present in their listening.

Your first step in developing mastery of this skill is to explore your own orientation toward the skill of appreciative listening. Reflect on the following questions:

• Is this skill important to you now?

• Is it worth working on?

• Given your role as participant, facilitator, or convener, what benefits might this skill provide to you?

• If this skill is not of primary importance to you now, what might you need to do to make it of primary importance?

• What might you do to increase the persistence and frequency of your listening?

Appreciative Listening Checklist #2

Notice the quality of your listening by using this checklist. Review the actions listed in the checklist and choose one to try in the moment to increase your skill.

Do I need to …

> … stop talking; take a vow of silence once in a while?
>
> … imagine the other person's viewpoint?
>
> … look, act, and be interested?
>
> … observe nonverbal behavior?
>
> … not interrupt; sit still past my tolerance level?
>
> … listen between the lines?
>
> … speak only affirmatively while listening?
>
> … ensure understanding through rephrasing key points?

APPLICATION:
ATTENDS TO PARTICIPANTS TO ENSURE ALL IDEAS AND
VOICES ARE HEARD

You are applying this skill when:

• *you are aware of filters that may influence what is heard and what is not heard for yourself and others.*

• *you use strategies to remain open, appreciative, and in the moment.*

• *you use nonverbal cues of attentiveness and interest.*

• *you ask Effective Questions to gain insight into assumptions, facts, and points of view and to verify understanding of what was said.*

In addition to working to be curious, open, and aware, you must also distinguish between what is being said and how you and others interpret it.

The following three exercises will heighten your awareness of this distinction.

PRACTICE: APPRECIATIVE LISTENING — FILTERS AND ASSOCIATIONS

Read the following story or have someone read it to you. As you read it or hear it, pay attention to what comes to mind.

> *The people had lived by the river for many, many years. The children learned from the elders every day. One of the elders had a special gift for telling stories, and the children loved to hear them.*
>
> *One of the children always listened very carefully to the beginning of every story, but would run away before the end. One day the elder asked the child, "Are you bored with the stories? Is that why you run away before the story ends?"*
>
> *And the child answered, "No — the stories are exciting. It's just that I know that even if you begin the story, it's up to me to find a way to end it!"*

As you were reading:

• What came to mind? Images? Associations?

• How might these images or associations reflect any experiences or assumptions that might be filters to your listening?

• For example, in your mind was the child a boy or a girl? Look again at the story; gender is not referenced. You may have a filter that led to you imagine a girl or boy.

• What images were evoked about the landscape? Urban? Rural? Suburban? In this country or another? In this time or another? You may have a filter that led you to imagine a specific time and place.

Make some notes to yourself about what you might keep in mind about listening and filters, and how you might use inquiry to explore meaning.

PRACTICE: APPRECIATIVE LISTENING — LISTENING IN A DIFFERENT WAY

Read and consider the quotation below. What might you do to listen in a way that is more appreciative, similar to the state of attention that is described?

I do not know if you have ever examined how you listen, it doesn't matter to what, whether to a bird, to the wind in the leaves, to the rushing waters, or how you listen in a dialogue with yourself, to your conversation in various relationships with intimate friends, your wife or husband ...

If we try to listen, we find it extraordinarily difficult, because we are always projecting our opinions and ideas, our prejudices, our background, our inclinations, our impulses; when they dominate, we hardly listen at all to what is being said ...

In that state there is no value at all. One listens and therefore learns, only in a state of attention, a state of silence, in which this whole background is in abeyance, is quiet; then, it seems to me, it is possible to communicate.

... real communication can only take place where there is silence.

— Jiddu Krishnamurti, from Talk and Dialogues, Saanen 1967,
  1st Public Talk July 9, 1967

Make some notes to yourself about what it means to include silence (listening) in the communication process.

PRACTICE: APPRECIATIVE LISTENING — DEMONSTRATING OPENNESS

In demonstrating appreciative listening, nonverbal cues are powerful. Your facial expression, your body language, the nod of your head, the look in your eye as you listen, all convey your spirit and intent to listen fully with nonjudgmental interest.

Comments and straightforward, Effective Questions also demonstrate openness and curiosity, and they create mutual understanding. Experiment with affirmative body language and comments, such as those below, in your conversations:

- Tell me more ...

- What leads you to that?

- Share more of your point of view ...

- How is what you are saying informed by your experience?

What are some other Effective Questions or statements that you use to demonstrate appreciative listening and create mutual understanding?

MASTERY: CONSISTENTLY DEMONSTRATES INTEREST IN CONVERSATIONS OF OTHERS THROUGHOUT THE MEETING

You are demonstrating mastery of this skill when:

- *you keep your own interests and interpretations in check (be neutral) when listening.*

- *you use a variety of strategies to engage the speaker (such as silence, nonverbal signals to encourage the speaker such as eye contact, or leaning toward the speaker).*

- *you quickly notice the lack of listening, acknowledge the lack, and self-correct.*

- *you maintain focused listening for the length of a meeting.*

Listening appreciatively makes people feel respected and known, which builds trust within the group. The increased awareness and understanding of differences in racial, cultural, socioeconomic, and ethnic backgrounds and experiences enables people of different backgrounds to understand and address tensions and conflicts.

Three Steps for Mastering Appreciative Listening[2]

Appreciative listening is enhanced by following a three-step process that focuses your attention.

STEP ONE: BECOME AWARE OF HOW YOU CURRENTLY LISTEN.

The first step is to create an awareness of how you currently listen to recognize what changes you need to make.

For example, people often filter what they hear in a conversation. At other times, we may not listen intently enough to distinguish between what is being said and our reaction. Sometimes we are not listening because we are thinking about what to say next. Perhaps the worst mistake people make is not listening because they have already made up their minds.

To become aware of your current listening behavior, notice the following:

- If you are listening or reacting

- What you appreciate about the speaker's words

- If you are thinking about what to say next

- If you are listening with an open mind

- If you are curious about what is being said

STEP TWO: RECOGNIZE WHAT TO LISTEN FOR.

As we listen, we not only receive information; we process it. We like what we hear or we don't like it. We agree or we disagree. Before drawing a conclusion, we can listen better by understanding what to listen for. Asking the following questions can help.

- What are my assumptions?
- What preconceived ideas do I bring to the discussion?

STEP THREE: USE OPEN-ENDED QUESTIONS TO LISTEN APPRECIATIVELY.

Once we begin to change the way we listen, we find that we are curious about the speaker's assumptions, facts, or point of view. This naturally leads us to gather more information or to inquire.

- What led the speaker to a specific conclusion?
- What is the speaker's line of reasoning?

Inquiry is an effective means of creating a dialogue in a nonthreatening way. It also makes your thinking more visible to others. The key to using questions well is not to judge, threaten, or attack the speaker.

- What leads you to conclude that?
- How does the proposal affect...?
- What things need to happen if...?
- How do you feel about...?

TIPS: MASTERING THE SKILL OF APPRECIATIVE LISTENING

DON'T TALK TOO MUCH
- Notice when people in the group are not talking or when you are talking more than the group.
- Then, you stop talking.
- Finally, you invite the group back with an Effective Question.

BE COMFORTABLE WITH SILENCE
- After asking an Effective Question, wait silently for the group to respond.
- Practice timing silence. Get comfortable with at least 15-30 seconds of silence.

USE BODY LANGUAGE
- Look expectantly at individuals.
- Read nonverbal cues from those who wish to speak.
- Send nonverbal cues, such as leaning into the group, moving close to the group, etc.

BREATHE AND FOCUS
- Use intentional, relaxed breathing to be fully present.
- When you notice a distracting thought or emotion, acknowledge it, and return to appreciative listening.
- Broaden your attention to include a focus on both the speakers and the listeners — holding awareness of the whole group.

ACKNOWLEDGE AND RETURN
- If you lose your ability to be appreciatively open, acknowledge your distraction from or reaction to the group and shift your attention back to appreciative listening.
- Invite the group to pause, breathe, and return to listening with you.
- If the group stops listening, label appreciative listening as an important ingredient for moving from talk to action, and invite the group to practice the skill in the interest of achieving meeting results.

PRACTICE: OPPORTUNITIES FOR APPRECIATIVE LISTENING

Developing the skill of appreciative openness can be done anywhere at any time. Answer the following questions to find opportunities to practice appreciative listening in your daily life.
- Where in your life do you think good-quality listening could make a difference?

In those times when you practiced good-quality listening, what changes did you notice in:
- the way you listened?
- the way those you were listening to spoke?
- the quality of the listening of the other people in the conversation?

Differential Impact: MBTI and Communication Preferences

You can deepen your mastery of appreciative openness by using MBTI awareness to understand people's communication preferences and hold more effective conversations. By paying attention to how people express themselves, you can make hypotheses about what they listen for, what they might explore through questions, and what type of relationship connection they prefer to establish. The table below provides information about the preferred mode of expression for each of the functional pairs.[3] When you hear people expressing themselves in one of these modes, test your hypotheses by noting what they listen for, and ask about what type of relationship connection they prefer.

FUNCTIONAL PAIRS AND COMMUNICATION

PAIR	MODE OF EXPRESSION	LISTENS FOR	ASKS ABOUT	PREFERRED RELATIONSHIP
SF	Uses personal pronouns; tells stories about why something is relevant personally	Personal impact and specific connections	Similarities in background, interests, and opinions	Established relationships are friendships; extends invitations to social gatherings and expects reciprocity
NF	Uses nonspecific words; likes to brainstorm, dream, and talk about possibilities	The possibilities or options that match a personal, idealized vision	Associations based on personal meaning, images, and feelings connected to personal visions	Wants relational harmony or the appearance of relational harmony; needs to feel listened to
ST	Uses impersonal words rather than personal pronouns	Specific facts, precision of language, logical comparisons	Step-by-step processes, objective criteria, data that test reliability of data and source	Accuracy builds trust; relationship does not necessarily involve sharing personal issues
NT	Uses impersonal pronouns and few personal references	Pros and cons, long-term factors, trends, and impact	What-if scenarios, problems, and difficulties	Knowledge and competency build trust; prefers business-like relationship

Your ability to listen for and use insights about people's communication preferences is strengthened by daily practice. The following exercise provides an opportunity to practice applying your understanding of MBTI communication preferences in conversations.

Review the communication preferences of the functional pairs in the table on the previous page.

Choose one or two people you work with frequently. Make hypotheses about their communication preferences.

Person #1:

Person #2:

The next time you are in conversation with them, listen to their mode of expression. Then use your hypotheses about their communication preferences to deepen the conversation and create a stronger connection between you and the shared work.

PARTICIPANT PRACTICE GUIDE 2.1:
DEMONSTRATE APPRECIATIVE OPENNESS

Appreciative listening is one aspect of the skill of demonstrating appreciative openness. Other aspects include using MBTI awareness of communication styles to modify how you communicate with others and being very attentive to both what people are saying and how people are listening to each other in meetings. All the aspects of appreciative openness can be used anywhere, anytime, and in any role.

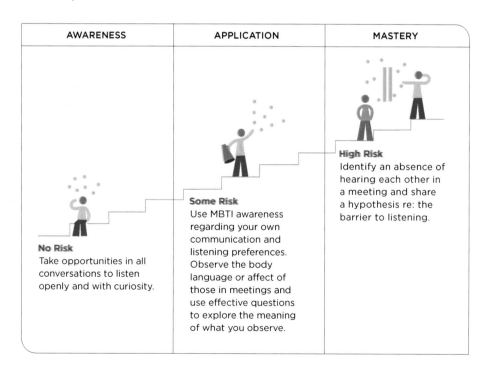

AWARENESS	APPLICATION	MASTERY
No Risk Take opportunities in all conversations to listen openly and with curiosity.	**Some Risk** Use MBTI awareness regarding your own communication and listening preferences. Observe the body language or affect of those in meetings and use effective questions to explore the meaning of what you observe.	**High Risk** Identify an absence of hearing each other in a meeting and share a hypothesis re: the barrier to listening.

SKILL 2.2: USE CONTEXT STATEMENTS, EFFECTIVE QUESTIONS AND LISTEN FORS

The skill of using a Context Statement, asking Effective Questions,[4] and listening with focused intent enables you to take what you are hearing and use that knowledge to frame dialogues. Framing dialogues makes it possible for people to be in the same conversation at the same time and use that common focus to address issues constructively. The three levels of this skill are described in the table below.

AWARENESS	APPLICATION	MASTERY
Understands and uses CS, EQs, LFs as a core technique for facilitating • *Do I set a context to focus a conversation on a meeting result?* • *Do I prepare EQs in advance to engage people, focus discussion, and move conversations forward toward meeting results?* • *Do I integrate a CS with an EQ and link it to an LF?*	Frames the work (purpose, focus, boundary) with a CS, EQ, and LF in the moment • *Do I use EQs (open ended, inquisitive) to engage people, focus conversations, and move conversations forward toward meeting results?* • *Do I listen for responses and incorporate them into the group's work by setting another CS and linked EQ?*	Regularly uses CS, EQs, and LFs to accelerate a group's ability to achieve meeting results • *Do I use CS, EQs, LFs to understand the group's experience of pace and adjust the pace to sustain maximum engagement?* • *Do I use awareness of differential impact (as informed by MBTI and B/ART) in CS, EQs, LFs?* • *Do I flexibly modify or change a CS, EQs, LFs in the moment based on my reading of the group?*
→	→	→

AWARENESS:
UNDERSTANDS AND USES CS, EQs, LFs AS CORE TECHNIQUE FOR FACILITATING

You are aware of this skill when:

• *you set a context to focus a conversation on a meeting result.*

• *you prepare EQs in advance to engage people, focus discussion, and move conversations forward toward meeting results.*

• *you integrate a CS with an EQ and link it to an LF.*

What you say to start a conversation and how you listen to a conversation can be practiced. The skill of making a Context Statement, asking an Effective Question, and knowing what to Listen For enables you and others to all be in the same focused conversation at the same time. The facilitator or participant can use these components together to frame and facilitate conversations.

PRACTICE: CS, EQs, AND LFs

> Your first step in developing mastery of this skill is to explore your own orientation. Reflect on the following questions:
>
> • Do I set the context using an easily understood statement?
>
> • Am I able to use Effective Questions to clarify and focus the discussion?
>
> • Am I able to identify Listen Fors?
>
> • Am I able to consciously hear what I am listening for?

The **Context Statement** helps people know what the conversation is about and helps them all be in the same conversation at the same time.

The purpose of this conversation is to identify what each person can contribute to the strategy.

The Context Statement signals to the participants what they want to accomplish in the conversation and how they will accomplish it. The CS gives a focus and sets a boundary for the conversation.

In this 10-minute conversation, you will have an opportunity to brainstorm ideas about what is contributing to the success of this program.

The **Effective Question** ignites the conversation and engages people in sharing information and listening to each other. Effective Questions are:

• open ended (i.e., not answered merely with yes or no)

• inquisitive (i.e., ask what or how?)

• you oriented (i.e., What do you think about ...? or How do you feel about ...?)

• appreciative (i.e., trusting that the person has the answer)

The **Listen For** is what you consciously have in mind to hear how people are responding to the Effective Question. In practicing the skill, be conscious of and able to name what you are listening for. For example, when people are responding to a question about what contributes to the success of a program, you are listening for concrete examples and specific ideas of the factors that make a program work well. In addition, you might be listening for the experiences that

CONTEXT STATEMENT
"The purpose of this conversation is to decide the agenda for our next meeting"

EFFECTIVE QUESTION
What do we need to do at our next meeting to move forward?

LISTEN FOR
• topics • issues
• decisions to be made

have shaped these ideas and how what they are suggesting connects to their image of program success.

The Listen For is an intentional filter held flexibly — never to block out what may not fit, but rather to focus on the essence of the conversation. A sharply tuned Listen For supports people and the group in hearing the heart of the matter more clearly. The skills of using Context Statement, Effective Questions, and Listen Fors are an integrated set.

Follow these tips to practice CS, EQ and LF skills.

TIPS: USING THE SKILLS OF CS, EQs, AND LFs

- Always state the context at the beginning of the conversation.

- Use the Effective Question as the header for the flip chart.

- Set up the chart format to display what you are listening for, e.g., if you are listening for examples as well as ideas, label the examples.

- Use your Listen For to determine if people are addressing the EQ or are on another topic.

- If people are addressing other questions or a different topic, create a separate flip chart as a parking lot for issues or conversations that are not focused on the EQ and/or within the context of the conversation.

- When necessary, use the parking lot to let the group members review and then choose which conversations they want to have when.

- Adjust the CS and the EQ in the moment to reflect those choices.

APPLICATION:
ATTENDS TO PARTICIPANTS TO ENSURE ALL IDEAS AND
VOICES ARE HEARD

You are applying this skill when:

- *you use EQs (open ended, inquisitive) to engage people, focus conversations, and move conversations forward toward meeting results.*

- *you Listen For responses and incorporate them into the group's work by setting another CS and linked EQ.*

Using the skills of setting a context, asking Effective Questions, and listening for key elements supports a group's capacity to stay engaged and listen appreciatively to each other. Optimum engagement is when the pace is just right — neither too slow nor too fast — and when the group as a whole is attentive and accepting of members' different paces. You can use Context Statement/Effective Questions/Listen Fors to optimize pace.

Address and Modulate the Pace

Context Statement: "Think of the meeting so far — from when we began to right now — and your experience of the meeting."

Effective Question: "Was it too fast?" (show of hands) "Too slow?" (show of hands) "Just right?" (show of hands)

Listen/Look For:[5] Watch and encourage the group to observe the different experiences of pace (how many feel the pace is too fast, too slow, just right).

Incorporate the Information and Adjust the CS, EQs, LFs to Move Forward

Invite the group to make observations about what the whole group experience is of the meeting's pace. If the group observation indicates a desire to adjust the pace:

Set a Context: Some members of the group think the meeting is too slow.

Ask an Effective Question: What do you think will work to adjust the pace?

Listen For proposals and ideas.

For meetings to move from talk to action, people must be clear about what they will do and when. An action commitment is a statement made by one or more participants conveying their intention to accomplish a task within a specific time frame. Action commitments may include tasks that are long term. Next steps complement action commitments by clarifying what needs to be accomplished in the short term. Action commitments and next steps used together increase the likelihood that tasks will get done. The following exercise offers Context Statements and Effective Questions to generate commitments to action and next steps.

Review the examples of Effective Questions for the two conversations below. Take the opportunity in an upcoming meeting to use Effective Questions about next steps and commitments to move the meeting to action and results.

NEXT STEPS

Context: This conversation is an opportunity to build on the results of the meeting.

- What are the next steps?

- What is the desired result of each next step?

- What makes the result important to the meeting participants?

- What is missing that would make the result possible?

- What can you see when the result is achieved? Who would notice?

- What does success look like? Who would celebrate success?

- What are the impact and/or consequence of achieving the result?

- What will you do next? What is the logic of that action; i.e., how will that action move you forward?

COMMITMENTS TO ACTION

Context: To achieve the next steps and actions, what are the specific promises made about who will do what, when, and with what impact?

- What is the sequence of the actions?

- With whom will you take action or connect?

- What will be done?

- What is the necessary action to move us forward?

- Who will do it?

- How will you do it?

- When will it begin and end?

- What is the impact of doing it?

- What are the consequences of not doing it?

- What is the backup plan if people can't do what they say they will do?

- What could prevent or be an obstacle to the action being taken?

- What relationships could remove or bypass the obstacle?

- What conversations are needed to create those relationships?

- What is needed for unequivocal commitment to taking action?

MASTERY:
REGULARLY USES CS, EQ, AND LF TO ACCELERATE A
GROUP'S ABILITY TO ACHIEVE MEETING RESULTS

You are demonstrating mastery of this skill when:

- *you use CS, EQ, and LF to understand the group's experience of pace and adjust the pace to sustain maximum engagement.*

- *you use awareness of differential impact (as informed by MBTI and B/ART) in CS, EQ, and LF.*

- *you flexibly modify or change a CS, EQ, and LF in the moment, based on the group's dynamics.*

Differential Impact: MBTI Functional Pairs Insights for EQs

MBTI functional pairs can inform the framing of Effective Questions by illuminating the type of questions that resonate with different preferences. The table below illustrates the context and EQs for each functional pair.

FRAMING EFFECTIVE QUESTIONS FOR DIFFERENT MBTI COMMUNICATION PREFERENCES

PAIR	PREFERRED CONTEXT	PREFERRED EQs
SF	Practical Information Personal Statements	Specifically, what would that look like? What is the impact on you?
NF	Feeling Statements Possibilities	What is that like? How is this unique?
ST	Factual, Sequential, Logical Impersonal Statements	What are the facts? How has this worked?
NT	Goals Options	Why? What if?

PARTICIPANT PRACTICE GUIDE 2.2:
USE CONTEXT STATEMENT, EFFECTIVE QUESTIONS, AND
LISTEN FORS

In your day-to-day work, you may notice that people are not in the same conversation at the same time. Using Context Statements, Effective Questions, and Listen Fors eliminates this confusion.

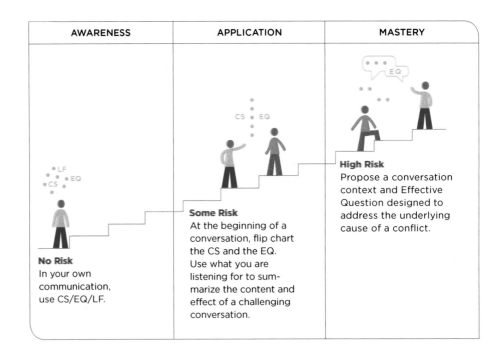

AWARENESS	APPLICATION	MASTERY
No Risk In your own communication, use CS/EQ/LF.	**Some Risk** At the beginning of a conversation, flip chart the CS and the EQ. Use what you are listening for to summarize the content and effect of a challenging conversation.	**High Risk** Propose a conversation context and Effective Question designed to address the underlying cause of a conflict.

NOTES:

[1] http://appreciativeinquiry.case.edu/uploads/whatisai.pdf is a helpful reference for Effective Questions that facilitate appreciative listening.

[2] Developed collaboratively with Phyllis Rozansky, a version originally appeared in the Center for the Study of Social Policy, *Learning Guides.*

[3] Brock. *Using Type in Selling: Building Customer Relationships with the Myers–Briggs Type Indicator.* Consulting Psychologists Press. 1994.

[4] Effective Questions were developed as a concept and skill by Oakley and Krug. The definition and many of the examples of Effective Questions can be found in *Leadership Made Simple.*

[5] Sometimes the Listen For is a Look For. The nonverbals convey the response.

HOLD GROUPS

**DEFINITION: SUPPORT GROUPS IN HAVING FOCUSED
CONVERSATIONS THAT MOVE TO RESULTS**

SKILLS FOR THIS COMPETENCY

3.1 USE FLIP CHART TO DISPLAY THE
GROUP'S WORK

3.2 SEQUENCE

3.3 SUMMARIZE

3.4 SYNTHESIZE

3.5 CHECK IN AND CHECK OUT

This chapter describes the Hold Groups competency.
This competency is made up of five skills that help
groups to be in the same conversation at the same time
with the capacity to track what is occurring and build
on ideas, move from idea to idea or segue from one
meeting result to another, and begin and end meetings
that move from talk to action. These skills include using
a flip chart to display the group's work; sequencing,
summarizing, and synthesizing; and checking in and
checking out.

》 **Differential impact:** people engaged in the same
conversation have varied reactions

SKILL 3.1: USE FLIP CHART TO DISPLAY THE GROUP'S WORK

Most people find it easier to focus on conversations if there is something visual that provides a focus. Flip charting (or using a white board) provides that focus by recording the key points of what is said, decisions, issues, options, and proposals.

Some key benefits of using a flip chart (or white board) are the following:

• Lets people know they've been heard.

• Provides a visible running record.

• Keeps everyone on track.

• Provides information to people who were not there (in the form of legible charts and/or typed notes of the charts).

• Reinforces that there is one conversation.

• Illuminates the context/Effective Question/Listen For of the conversation.

• Allows a group to choose among and sequence multiple conversations or topics.

• Organizes information to support summary and synthesis.

The table below defines the skill of flip charting and provides questions to assess your current skill level. Knowing your current skill level allows you to focus your practice and move to mastery.

AWARENESS	APPLICATION	MASTERY
Displays group's work accurately	Displays group's work to focus on meeting results	Displays group's work to accelerate progress toward achieving meeting results
• Do people read what is captured? Is it accurate?	• Do my charts serve as a tool to recap work for summary?	• Do my charts support the building of proposals and making decisions?
• Do I use the Context Statement, Effective Questions and Listen Fors to inform what is captured?	• Do I use techniques (color, underlining, symbols, spacing, lines) to highlight, track, and distinguish conversations?	• Does my charting support synthesis and movement toward meeting results?
• Does the speaker recognize what was said in what I captured?	• Do people who were not in the conversation know its content from what is charted?	• Do my charts support accountability for action during and after the meeting?
• Do I easily capture parallel conversations and accurately record decisions?	• Do group members look at and refer to my charts?	

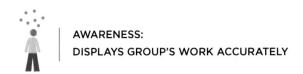

AWARENESS:

DISPLAYS GROUP'S WORK ACCURATELY

You are aware of this skill when:

- *you see people read what is captured.*

- *you know the charting is accurate.*

- *you realize the CS, EQs, and LFs inform what is captured.*

- *you know the speaker recognizes what was said in what is captured.*

Flip charting requires knowledge and practice. The tips on the next page outline some of the things you can do to make your flip charts not only legible but also useful to group.

TIPS: USING THE FLIP CHART TO DISPLAY THE GROUP'S WORK ACCURATELY

USE THE PROPER TOOLS AND TECHNIQUE

The basic tools are colored markers, flip chart pads, easels, and tape.

- Keep all the recorder's tools in a special box or tote bag so you don't forget anything.

- Make sure that whatever is being recorded is clearly visible to the whole group. For example, if possible, use alternating dark colors to separate ideas, and only use red or light colors for emphasis. (Red and light colors are difficult for some people to read across the room.)

- Use wide or wedge-tipped markers for thicker lines and leave ample white space.

- Make the letters at least 2–3 inches tall, and leave white space between lines and words.[1]

WORK EFFECTIVELY WITH THE GROUP

- Listen hard at all times.

- Remain neutral. When you pick up the marker, you are picking up the neutral role. Also, by passing the marker to someone else so he or she can record when you are not neutral, you build the capacity of the group to do its work.

- Ask the group to repeat or clarify as necessary.

- Accept corrections graciously.

- If you are co-facilitating and charting for another facilitator, use the Context Statement/Effective Questions/Listen Fors of the facilitator to organize the information on the chart.

- Always put the Context Statement or Effective Questions at the top of the chart to focus the group's conversation. Use Listen Fors to label what is being captured.

- Take the opportunity to gesture toward the flip chart or point out what is recorded to support the group's focus.

DECIDE WHAT TO RECORD

- Write down what is often called the group memory. Depending on the specific meeting result, group memory can include questions, answers, insights, concerns, feedback, and ideas from brainstorming sessions. Always record decisions and commitments of who will do what when.

- If in doubt, it's all right to ask something like, "Should I be writing that down?" or "How can I best capture that on paper?" The idea is to work with the group to help you decide what to record.

RECORD EFFECTIVELY

- Write in large letters, legibly, and quickly. Put headers on each sheet and number your sheets.

- Don't try to write every word. Use abbreviations recognizable to the group and don't write small words like "the." Write mainly nouns and verbs.

- Only paraphrase when you are confident the speaker will recognize the paraphrasing. Do not paraphrase as a way to avoid writing controversial statements. Charting helps a group see and address differences and disagreements.

- Don't attribute points to individuals (i.e., do not write down names) unless attribution is important to the work (e.g., who will do what).

- Be sensitive to cultural norms and boundaries of civility. Acknowledge when you are not capturing information to respect the norms of civil discourse or the group.

- Don't worry about spelling. You can write the sp symbol by any word you are unsure of or invite the group to edit your charts later.

- Use color, symbols, and underlining to highlight points. Make clear when there is a list of topics or ideas that can support a summary.

APPLICATION:
DISPLAYS GROUP'S WORK TO FOCUS ON MEETING RESULTS

You are applying this skill when:

- *you utilize charts as a tool to recap work.*

- *you use color, underlining, symbols, spacing, and lines to highlight, track, and distinguish conversations.*

- *you realize people who were not in the conversation know its content from what is charted.*

- *you see group members look at and refer to the charts.*

Take the opportunities in daily life to develop mastery. Dos and Don'ts for flip charting are on the next page.

DO

- Use your flip chart as a reference for topics, ideas, and decisions.

- Refer to the flip chart when offering a summary and invite your co-facilitator to do the summary or add to the one you have offered.

- Summarize all decisions, and check the accuracy with the group.

- Respectfully bring to the speakers' awareness what conversation they are in, and inquire whether they want the group to discuss that topic or stay with the current topic. Offer to place the new topic on another chart.

- Ask if a participant would like to summarize or synthesize.

- Use more than one flip chart to separate ideas, conversations, or options. Use a parking lot flip chart to hold topics or ideas for later discussion.

- Use the flip chart to capture commitments to action and ensure that the group answers the questions of who, what, and when for each commitment.

DON'T

- Don't ignore the visual aid of the flip chart.

- Don't ignore what your co-facilitator or the group has to offer.

- Don't assume everyone has the same idea of what the group has decided.

- Don't ignore speakers who are not speaking to the topic being charted.

- Don't ignore the wisdom in the group.

- Don't confuse or conflate topics or ideas.

- Don't ignore the need for groups to make commitments to move to action

MASTERY:
DISPLAYS GROUP'S WORK TO ACCELERATE PROGRESS
TOWARD ACHIEVING MEETING RESULTS

You are demonstrating mastery of this skill when:

- *you see the group use charts to build proposals and make decisions.*

- *you see that charting supports synthesis and accelerates the group's work.*

- *you confirm that charts are used to support accountability for action during and after the meeting.*

Flip charting at the mastery level helps groups make meaning of free-flowing conversations, see more clearly the choices to be made, and see and address barriers to commitment to action and accountability for results. The key to mastery is the capacity to listen to a free-flowing group conversation and capture the essence of the conversation in a way that allows the group to see the content of the conversation, then decide together what to do to move the conversation forward.

WHEN YOU HEAR ...	CAPTURE ...	GIVE WORK BACK TO THE GROUP BY SAYING...
People advocating for different ideas and trying to convince each other through argument	Capture each idea on a separate flip chart or portion of a flip chart and label the ideas as options	The group is considering different options. • What are the strengths of each? • What are the differences of each? • Are there other options that can move the group forward?
An emergent theme or organizing idea that brings parts of a conversation together into a larger whole	Capture the idea in a succinct phrase or draw a picture where people can see the parts of the conversation as part of a bigger concept or idea	Does this phrase (or picture) capture what is emerging in this conversation? • Would you like to modify it to more completely reflect your work? • If it captures your work, how can you build on it to support the group going forward?
People talking about what should happen	Draw a chart with the headers What, Who, When, Impact	The group is beginning to think about action. • Who will take that action? When? • What do you want to see or have happen as the result of that action (impact)?

Flip charting helps groups carry on one conversation at a time. The following exercise develops a practice plan for flip charting.

PRACTICE: SKILL DEVELOPMENT

Take a piece of paper and draw a vertical line down the middle. Label the left column Obstacles and the right column Opportunities. Use the example EQs and LFs listed below to elicit both the obstacles and the opportunities you see, and how those obstacles might be opportunities to solve problems or address barriers to you developing mastery in flip charting. After answering the question, you can compare your answers to the examples provided. The opportunities to develop skill identified through this exercise become your flip-charting practice plan.

OBSTACLES	OPPORTUNITIES
EQ #1: What are all the obstacles to your achieving mastery level in flip charting?	EQ #2: As you consider each obstacle, what is the opportunity embedded in the obstacle?
LF #1: List the specifics that clarify when, how, and where the obstacle occurs.	LF #2: List the specifics that show how you can change an attitude, practice a skill, or create a new circumstance.
Example obstacles to flip charting: • Not sure what to write down. • Often can't tell what is important and what is not. • Not sure how much or how little to capture.	Example opportunities embedded in the obstacles: • Practice Listen Fors in informal conversations while taking notes for yourself. • Review your notes and see if you captured in an abbreviated way enough information so that someone who was not in the conversation would know the most important content. • Practice until you are confident that you are capturing the minimum needed to help people know what occurred in the conversation and build on it.

The Co-Facilitator Role

Groups in complex or fast-moving conversations can often benefit from two people supporting the group — one as a facilitator and the other as a co-facilitator charting the conversation. Another dimension of mastery is to be able work well with or as a co-facilitator. The following are suggested steps that a co-facilitator can take to ensure that the partnership supports the work of the group well.

BEFORE YOU BEGIN

The facilitator and co-facilitator review the desired meeting results and, for each meeting result, clarify the Context Statement, discuss possible Effective Questions, and focus on what to Listen For. The co-facilitator then is prepared to structure the flip charts to best capture the CS/EQs/LFs.

The facilitator and co-facilitator agree on how to work together. The agreement is specific about if and when a co-facilitator, in addition to charting, might call to attention a comment that the facilitator might not have heard; make a comment or observation about group dynamics; publicly or privately comment or intervene if the facilitator has fallen out of the neutral role; or take the role of referring to the flip chart and then offering the summary or synthesis.

WHILE CO-FACILITATING

If the co-facilitator hasn't heard a statement, he or she can check with the facilitator to verify the accuracy of the charts. The co-facilitator can also check with the participant to affirm the accuracy of what is captured on the charts.

The co-facilitator is an extra set of eyes; e.g., someone has a hand raised or has made a nonverbal gesture that the facilitator did not see. The co-facilitator may say something like, "Bob, I think Caroline wants to join the conversation."

While charting, the co-facilitator manages his or her nonverbal behavior so as not to distract the group from the conversation.

If the co-facilitator steps out of charting role to make a comment, it's important to visibly turn the meeting over to the lead facilitator. (Returning to the co-facilitator role doesn't have to be verbal — just fade into the background.)

 PARTICIPANT PRACTICE GUIDE 3.1:
USE FLIP CHART TO DISPLAY THE GROUP'S WORK

Charting is a quintessential task for facilitators. Charting is so central to the role that holding the marker and standing by a flip chart is the signal of who holds the facilitator role. However, participants can also use charting as long as when they are charting they are also holding the neutral facilitator role. Therefore, when you are charting, your point of view is not informing the conversation.

In order to practice the skill without losing the opportunity to add your point of view to the conversation, consider choosing to chart for a brief period of time and then asking another participant to chart while you add your point of view to the conversation. Another opportunity would be to chart when there is a conversation that does not require you to voice your point of view. The following guide gives examples of how to practice charting in the participant role in situations where it is appropriate for you to hold the neutral role.

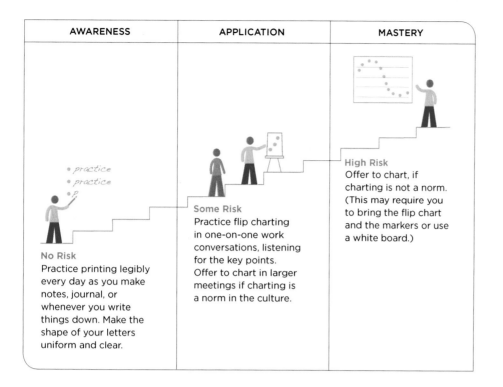

AWARENESS	APPLICATION	MASTERY

No Risk
Practice printing legibly every day as you make notes, journal, or whenever you write things down. Make the shape of your letters uniform and clear.

Some Risk
Practice flip charting in one-on-one work conversations, listening for the key points. Offer to chart in larger meetings if charting is a norm in the culture.

High Risk
Offer to chart, if charting is not a norm. (This may require you to bring the flip chart and the markers or use a white board.)

The three skills of sequencing, summarizing, and synthesizing support groups in holding focused conversations that have a beginning, a middle, and an end and that build toward a result. Conversation results are the products of a group holding a common task together. These skills are important for facilitators and co-facilitators — for example, a facilitator will often turn to the co-facilitator and ask for a summary or synthesis or to share the topics "in play" and ask the group to propose a sequence. Similarly, these skills can be very helpful when used by participants.

For example, if the task is brainstorming ideas, then the conversation result is a full and expansive list of ideas that reflect the contributions of all members, not limited by any member's preconceived ideas or critical judgment. The Hold 3R Meetings competency chapter of this book further explores the broad range of conversation results and how those results add up to meeting results that allow groups to move from talk to action.

SKILL 3.2: SEQUENCE

Groups often circle, spin, and frustrate themselves because people cannot get their voices into the conversation, because multiple conversations are occurring at the same time, or because the group members can't organize their conversations so they can take steps that build toward a conversation or meeting result. Establishing a sequence of speakers, conversations, and work helps groups move forward together.

The table below defines the skill of sequencing and describes that skill at three levels of development. Use the questions to assess your current skill level and focus your practice on the specific skills needed to move you along the path to mastery.

AWARENESS	APPLICATION	MASTERY
Understands and practices sequencing speakers • *Do I establish who speaks when in a way that is clear to the group and enables participants to relax and listen?*	Understands and practices sequencing topics or ideas • *Do I recognize different topics or conversations, label them, and invite the group to choose which conversation to have when?*	Understands and practices sequencing the work of meetings and meeting results • *Do I recognize opportunities for proposals, decisions, and commitments to action and invite the group to sequence them during the meeting to accomplish meeting results?*
→	→	→

AWARENESS:

UNDERSTANDS AND PRACTICES SEQUENCING SPEAKERS

You are aware of this skill when:

• *you establish who speaks when in a way that is clear to the group and enables participants to relax and listen.*

Sequencing Speakers

People can only attend to one voice at a time. Ask that those who want to speak raise their hands. Make a list of speakers and call them in order — or, more informally, give them numbers and have them remember their number in the sequence.

After establishing a sequence, ask if anyone else wants to speak. Watch for nonverbal cues and respond with a nonverbal acknowledgment (such as a nod) to let people know they are in the sequence. Build the group's confidence by assuring people that they will be able to pay attention to the conversation and not have to worry about whether they will get an opportunity to speak.

Sometimes certain members do not respect the sequencing — perhaps breaking in on other speakers and/or speaking out of turn. How the facilitator responds to out-of-sequence participation varies based on the context and the group culture. However, here are some factors that can inform the facilitator's response:

- Often group members with high levels of hierarchical authority test the facilitator's authority. The facilitator's role is to treat all group members as equals, and therefore, the preferred response is to work to hold the sequence and acknowledge when the sequence of speakers, e.g., someone of higher authority speaking whenever they want or "out of turn," is not accepted.

- Extroverted, highly engaged, or argumentative members may ignore sequence as they respond to every comment or idea offered. The facilitator works to hold back their comments (Do you mind waiting until X or Y has spoken?) and tests whether the group wants to pause the sequence to have a deeper conversation on the issue under discussion.

- Aggrieved or hostile members may ignore sequence. The facilitator can attend to the underlying intent of the comments and use inquiry to identify the source of the conflict and support the group's capacity to directly address the conflict.

APPLICATION:
UNDERSTANDS AND PRACTICES SEQUENCING TOPICS OR IDEAS

You are applying this skill when:

- *you recognize different topics or conversations, label them, and invite the group to choose which conversation to have when.*

In addition to working to be curious, open, and aware, you must also distinguish between what is being said and how you and others interpret it.

Sequencing Topics with EQs

To help groups sequence their topics, you may want to say, "I think you are having more than one conversation at the same time." List the topics, then ask the following EQs:

- Do you want to continue in multiple conversations, or would you like to propose a sequence?

- What conversations are you having?

- Which conversation would you like to have now?

- Is there a topic that needs to be discussed first before you can make a decision or move forward?

MASTERY:
UNDERSTANDS AND PRACTICES SEQUENCING THE WORK
OF MEETINGS AND MEETING RESULTS

You are demonstrating mastery of this skill when:

- *you recognize opportunities for proposals, decisions, and commitments to action and invite the group to sequence them to accomplish meeting results.*

Sequencing the Work of the Group

Sometimes people need to review and read before they can engage in a conversation. Offer people library time to read material before the conversation begins.

Conversations are often more focused if people reflect first (make notes, jot down thoughts) before sharing their thoughts aloud. Offer people a few moments to reflect before the conversation begins.

If there are sidebar conversations, find out if smaller conversations are needed before the larger conversation can begin. Be appreciative. All conversations are valuable; however, there can only be one at a time.

Groups often discover that they do not have the information they need to move forward or that the people who need to address certain issues are absent. Label the missing information and/or people and invite the group to decide how to move forward. Examples of typical options for moving forward include tabling issues until the necessary information or people are present and moving on to other work, discussing how to get the information or the people, or conducting preliminary conversations with a commitment to revisit the topic when the information or people are available.

A less common (though often productive) option is for the facilitator to help the group acknowledge that the work cannot be accomplished and agree to end the meeting immediately with one of two actions:

- A commitment to gather the information or connect with absent members.

- An agreement that the work will not get done at all and a commitment to deal with the consequences.

People are often frustrated in meetings because they can't get their voices heard in the conversation. Sequencing helps all voices be heard. This Participant Practice Guide offers approaches for using the skill of sequencing in your daily work in a way that will alleviate frustration and produce more engaged and productive conversations.

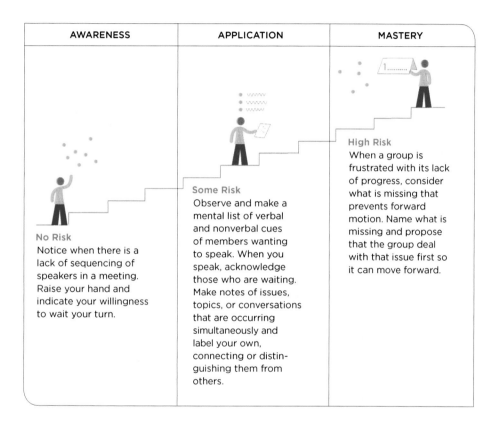

AWARENESS	APPLICATION	MASTERY
No Risk Notice when there is a lack of sequencing of speakers in a meeting. Raise your hand and indicate your willingness to wait your turn.	**Some Risk** Observe and make a mental list of verbal and nonverbal cues of members wanting to speak. When you speak, acknowledge those who are waiting. Make notes of issues, topics, or conversations that are occurring simultaneously and label your own, connecting or distinguishing them from others.	**High Risk** When a group is frustrated with its lack of progress, consider what is missing that prevents forward motion. Name what is missing and propose that the group deal with that issue first so it can move forward.

SKILL 3.3: SUMMARIZE

For groups to move from talk to action, they need to know where they are in a conversation to figure out how to move to the next step. When engaged fully in a conversation, group members may forget or lose track of the thread, so they would find it helpful to have a list of ideas shared, options identified, or decisions made. The table below describes the skill of summarizing at the three levels of development.

AWARENESS	APPLICATION	MASTERY
Remembers and can list ideas from short conversations • *Do I have a way to practice hearing, accurately remembering, and restating a list of ideas that emerges from a conversation?*	Remembers and can list categories of topics from medium to long conversations • *Do I concisely and accurately describe the content of conversations?* • *Do my summaries move a group forward toward the meeting results?*	Remembers and can briefly list process description or meeting results from a whole meeting • *Do I mentally review and then concisely state what has occurred in the meeting and the results achieved?*

AWARENESS:
REMEMBERS AND CAN LIST IDEAS FROM SHORT CONVERSATIONS

You are aware of this skill when:

• *you can hear, accurately remember, and restate as a list the ideas that emerge from a conversation.*

PRACTICE: SUMMARIZING

> Summarizing a list of ideas is possible when you are conscious of what you are listening for and stay focused on ideas while listening for the length of a whole conversation. Think about how well you currently summarize ideas:
>
> • How well do you summarize ideas now?
>
> • Can you readily list ideas you have heard?
>
> • What is a practice you might adopt to strengthen your ability to summarize ideas?

Here is an example of an exercise that helps you hear and accurately restate ideas:

1. In a conversation, make a mental note of what you are listening for.

2. As you hear examples of what you are listening for, mentally give that example a number.

3. Keep track of how many examples are in your mental list.

4. Begin your summary by stating what you were listening for and the number of ideas you heard. For example, in this conversation, I heard five ideas about how to invite new members to our group. One...

APPLICATION:
REMEMBERS AND CAN LIST CATEGORIES OF TOPICS
FROM MEDIUM TO LONG CONVERSATIONS

You are applying this skill when:

- *you concisely and accurately describe the content of conversations.*

- *you summarize in a way that moves a group forward toward the meeting results.*

Types of summaries that can help a group move from talk to action include:

- A summary of meeting results accomplished up to that point. This helps the group see what it needs to do next.

- A summary of similarities and differences in perspectives or points of view. This helps the group work toward convergence, or agree to disagree. A process that supports this summary includes five steps:

  1. Indicate that you are going to summarize the group's differences and similarities.

  2. Summarize the differences.

  3. Summarize the similarities.

  4. Ask for confirmation: Have I got it right?

  5. Invite the group to identify areas of agreement or common ground.

- A summary of issues, challenges, pros, cons, and feelings.

- A summary of decisions and commitments to action.

TIPS: SUMMARIZING

DO

- Practice naming and capturing as separate lists the different ideas associated with each topic.

- Ask group members to add to a summary.

- Summarize all points of view, even those only held by a few or those that may cause discomfort or generate conflict.

- Make notes to yourself or use a flip chart to ensure you can list all related items in a summary.

- Be brief in your summary; list the highlights of the work and skip the details.

- Move from summary to synthesis when the group is ready to move forward.

DON'T

- Don't lose track of what people are saying.

- Don't ignore what the group has to offer.

- Don't conveniently forget the points of view that are in the minority or cause the group discomfort.

- Don't trust your unaided memory.

- Don't bog down the group in reliving the whole conversation.

- Don't focus on the parts when the group is ready to work with the whole.

MASTERY:

REMEMBERS AND CAN BRIEFLY LIST PROCESS DESCRIPTION OR MEETING RESULTS FROM A WHOLE MEETING

You are demonstrating mastery of this skill when:

- *you mentally review and concisely state what has occurred in the meeting and the results achieved.*

Mastery requires developing the capacity to remember and list decisions or processes from meetings that may last anywhere from an hour or two to one or more days. Summary at the mastery level is strengthened by consciously working to know what to look for, categorizing what is happening, and holding the memory in a coherent way that enables summary.

When practicing for this level of mastery, develop a repertoire of Listen Fors that capture the life of meetings. For example, always listen for decisions and, as you listen, attach the decision mentally to the moment the decision was made and how the participants made the decision. This Listen For will enable you to summarize all decisions made during a meeting.

PARTICIPANT PRACTICE GUIDE 3.3:
SUMMARIZE

One-to-one conversations, conference calls, and meetings can provide many opportunities to build your summarizing skill. The following Participant Practice Guide gives examples of low-risk to high-risk methods; begin with the no- to low-risk techniques. As you gain confidence and mastery, experiment with the higher-risk options.

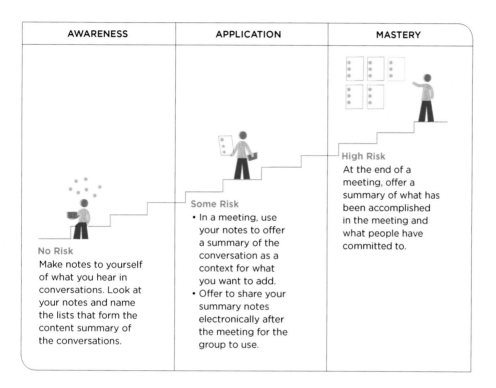

AWARENESS	APPLICATION	MASTERY

No Risk
Make notes to yourself of what you hear in conversations. Look at your notes and name the lists that form the content summary of the conversations.

Some Risk
• In a meeting, use your notes to offer a summary of the conversation as a context for what you want to add.
• Offer to share your summary notes electronically after the meeting for the group to use.

High Risk
At the end of a meeting, offer a summary of what has been accomplished in the meeting and what people have committed to.

SKILL 3.4: SYNTHESIZE

This skill brings the parts of a conversation or meeting together and offers a thread of common meaning that represents the whole. Synthesis combines the parts into a unified whole; synthesis gets at the heart of the matter.

Synthesizing is a more advanced skill than summarizing. Summarizing compiles or lists what occurred. Summarizing requires attention, memory, and focus.

To synthesize, however, requires a way to name, organize, or identify conversations or meeting results so that people can see the parts as a whole and can use that insight to move forward. Synthesizing is a step beyond summarizing, though the ability to summarize informs the synthesis.

The table below defines and describes the skill of synthesizing. Answering the questions provides you with an assessment of your current skill level and points you toward practices that build your ability.

AWARENESS	APPLICATION	MASTERY
Briefly states the meaning of short conversations • *Do I listen for the central meaning of the conversation and state that concisely?* • *Do I use basic methods of synthesis (comparison, themes, part/whole connections) in listening for and concisely stating where the group is in their work?*	Integrates and briefly states the meaning of a number of conversations or longer conversations • *Does the group affirm my synthesis and use it to move forward to meeting results?* • *Do I use images and symbolism to help the group own the results of a whole meeting?*	Integrates and briefly states the meaning for a whole meeting • *Does my synthesis accelerate the group's work?* • *Does the group use my synthesis to move to action?*
→	→	→

AWARENESS:
BRIEFLY STATES THE MEANING OF SHORT CONVERSATIONS

You are aware of this skill when:

- *you listen for the central meaning of the conversation and state that concisely.*

- *you use basic methods of synthesis (comparison, themes, part/whole connections) in listening for and concisely stating where the group is in its work.*

Your perception of the central meaning of a conversation can be influenced by MBTI preferences. You can strengthen your capacity to synthesize by knowing what your focus is and what you value, and then intentionally listening for aspects of meaning in conversation that reflect the focus and values of other MBTI preferences.[2] The table on the next page illustrates the focus and what the people with the functional pair value.

FOCUS AND VALUE FOR EACH FUNCTIONAL PAIR

PAIRS	FOCUS	VALUE
SF	The impact on people of specific facts	Loyalty and maintaining relationships
NF	How the big picture/general concept (not specifics) impacts people or supports their values	Making a difference in the community, for the family, for the world
ST	The logical implication of specific facts	Acting responsibly
NT	How the big picture possibilities create logical options	Competent pursuit of options that meet current and future needs

APPLICATION:
INTEGRATES AND BRIEFLY STATES THE MEANING FOR
A NUMBER OF CONVERSATIONS OR LONGER CONVERSATIONS

You are applying this skill when:

- *the group affirms your synthesis and uses it to move forward to meeting results.*

- *you use images and symbolism to help the group own the results of a whole meeting.*

TIPS: SYNTHESIZING

DO

- Go to the balcony and ask yourself, "What is the conversation about?" This balcony observation will allow you to begin to "listen for" the heart of the matter. Treat your answer as a preliminary hypothesis.

- Always say that you are offering a synthesis to help the group move forward; check to see if the group agrees.

- Give the work back to the group by inviting people to take a moment to reflect on the whole conversation and its meaning. Then ask, "Would someone like to offer a synthesis?"

- Chart to support the synthesis by drawing a picture that fits the parts into a whole. Practice using graphic images that represent part/whole relationships, such as diagrams with arrows connecting one part to another.

- Use metaphors or symbols to express the essence of what the whole group is feeling about the work.

- Offer the marker to participants who might want to draw pictures or images of how the parts of a conversation form a larger whole.

- Develop a repertoire of mental models to enrich your hypotheses about the meaning of a conversation. Examples of mental models can be found in Book Two.

DON'T

- Don't ignore other interpretations of what the conversation is about.

- Don't ignore what the group has to offer.

- Don't move so quickly that people do not have time to reflect on the meaning of the whole.

- Don't ignore the value of creating a visual representation of the parts and the whole.

- Don't forget that emotion and mood inform the capacity of the group to work together and move to action.

- Don't use the authority of the charter or the facilitator to impose meaning.

- Don't ignore the implicit mental models that the group may be using.

MASTERY:
CAN INTEGRATE AND BRIEFLY STATE THE MEANING FOR A WHOLE MEETING

You are demonstrating mastery of this skill when:

- *your synthesis accelerates the group's work.*

- *the group uses your synthesis to move to action.*

The following exercise is designed to help you identify imagery or symbolism in conversations.

Take note of when people use imagery or symbolism in conversations. Identify to yourself the sources of that imagery or symbolism. The following are examples of sources of imagery or symbolism that you may hear in conversations:

Current events: In the aftermath of Hurricane Katrina, the images of the disaster came to symbolize inadequate response to need.

Quotes from well-known sources: A quote from Shakespeare or a verse from the Bible may convey a powerful image.

Familiar stories: References to movies, plays, TV shows, novels, or historical events may be interpretations of the meaning of a conversation or a meeting.

Consider your sources of imagery and symbolism. As you listen to conversations, make associations to those sources, share them, and see how they resonate with the group.

Synthesis at the mastery level moves people to action by enabling the group as a whole to grasp the meaning of the work and move it forward. The table below offers some common methods of synthesis[3] and offers practices that help you apply the method in conversations.

METHODS FOR SYNTHESIS

METHOD	DESCRIPTION OF PRACTICE
Narratives or stories	Practice using the architecture of stories in the moment to create a short story of the meaning of a conversation or a meeting. The following EQs can help you create the narrative. Express that narrative in a sentence or two. • What kind of a story is this? Drama? Romance? Adventure? • Who are the protagonists? Band of brothers? Kind-hearted Samaritans? • What is the beginning, the middle, and the end?
Taxonomies or classification systems	Practice using classification systems as your Listen Fors in conversations. Use what you have categorized to inform a brief synthesis in the context of the classification system. Here are a couple of examples of Listen Fors based on classification systems from different disciplines: • domains of learning and stages of development (education) • market conditions, investment opportunities, risk, and return on investment (business)
Complex concepts	Practice using concepts that can be represented as diagrams to chart information so that the group can generate a synthesis. The following are examples of concepts from the quality improvement field that are easy to chart and support group synthesis: • A fishbone diagram synthesizes multiple activities and their sequencing to achieve a result. A fishbone diagram sequences events along a timeline to show cause and effect relationships. • A scatter plot graph synthesizes multiple data points into meaningful patterns. A scatter plot graph displays information using the two axes of the graph to show the correlation of two variables.

Take opportunities in meetings and conversations to use one of these methods to develop syntheses that are brief and clear and that support movement to action.

PARTICIPANT PRACTICE GUIDE 3.4:
SYNTHESIZE

Take the opportunity to synthesize many times a day. In conversations, practice seeing the parts as a whole, naming the whole briefly, and expressing the essence of the whole.

To reach the mastery level, you need to practice extensively in many different types of conversations before you have the experience necessary to synthesize more complex conversations in meetings. Begin with no-risk situations, and as you gain confidence in your mastery of the skill move to using synthesis in higher-risk situations.

Accelerate your development of this skill by noticing the impact on the group of your synthesis. Note which of your syntheses tend to be used by other participants and if the synthesis moves the group forward. Attending to the impact of your syntheses provides you with the information to make your syntheses more powerful and accessible.

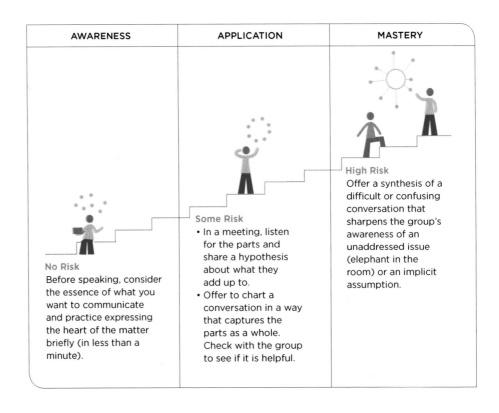

AWARENESS	APPLICATION	MASTERY
No Risk Before speaking, consider the essence of what you want to communicate and practice expressing the heart of the matter briefly (in less than a minute).	**Some Risk** • In a meeting, listen for the parts and share a hypothesis about what they add up to. • Offer to chart a conversation in a way that captures the parts as a whole. Check with the group to see if it is helpful.	**High Risk** Offer a synthesis of a difficult or confusing conversation that sharpens the group's awareness of an unaddressed issue (elephant in the room) or an implicit assumption.

SKILL 3.5: CHECK IN AND CHECK OUT

Conversations and meetings have beginnings, middles, and ends. For conversations and meetings to be effective, people need to be joined to the work and to each other. They need to acknowledge the endings of conversations and meetings to transition to the next step of taking the action between meetings.

The skill of checking in (joining to the work) and checking out (transitioning to the next step) is used at the beginning and ending of meetings, respectively, and also during meetings to ensure that people are moving together from conversation to conversation or from one type of work to another.

The check-in can be as short as each person saying a brief sentence or a phrase or a word. A check-out similarly can be brief. Conversely check-ins and check-outs may be longer and more in-depth. The content and the length of the check-in and check-out are varied, depending on what is needed for the group to advance its work.

As you develop mastery in this skill, you will experiment and find uses for this skill that are responsive to the needs and expectations of the group.

CHECK-IN	CHECK-OUT
A process to facilitate connections to the task and with others so people are ready to work together.	A process to facilitate the closing of a meeting so people are committed to the group, ready to transition to follow up, and aware of the progress made toward their own results and the meeting results.

The table on the next page describes the skill of checking in and checking out. The questions assess your current skill level and offer practice methods to build your ability to use check-in and check-out effectively. Practice using check-in at the beginning of meetings to frame the meeting results, and use check-out at the end to move to action. At the mastery level, using check-in and check-out reliably joins people to each other and the work and enables groups to consistently move from talk to action.

AWARENESS	APPLICATION	MASTERY
Understands and uses check-in and check-out • *Does my check-in establish a foundation for the group to own the achievement of meeting results?* • *Do my check-outs assess meeting results and move people to action?*	Connects group members to each other and the meeting results • *Do I consider the relationships of the people to each other and the work in framing the check-in and check-out?* • *Do my check-ins and check-outs illuminate B/ART and make it more likely that members will contribute their resources to the meeting results?* • *Do my check-outs address whether meeting results were achieved and elicit how group members felt about the meeting experience?*	Reads group to inform check-in and check-out • *Do I use the technique of checking in and out flexibly during a series of conversations or to facilitate transitions from one meeting result to another?* • *Do I use check-in or check-out to explore hypotheses about group dynamics or make the group aware of group dynamics?* • *Do my check-ins and check-outs at the beginning and end of meetings and the beginning and end of conversations move a group to action?*

AWARENESS:

UNDERSTANDS AND USES CHECK-IN AND CHECK-OUT

You are aware of this skill when:

• *your check-in establishes a foundation for the group to own the achievement of meeting results.*

• *your check-out assesses meeting results and moves people to action.*

Check-Ins

Check-ins are ignited with a brief Context Statement (CS) that names the purpose of the check-in and launches with an Effective Question (EQ) that touches on the relational and task dimensions that need to be addressed during the meeting. A check-in can consist of more than one EQ to bring these multiple dimensions into the awareness of the group and strengthen the group's ability to work together. Up to three or four questions can be posed to the group to frame the check-in. After providing a moment for reflection, each participant includes in his or her check-in statement responses to all three or four questions. It is good practice to provide a brief summary or synthesis of a more complex check-in as a segue to the work of the meeting.

A standard check-in that integrates relational and task dimensions is one that uses three Effective Questions to connect people to each other and to the work. Known as PIT Check-In, it provides a rapid method to begin a meeting with people ready to work together.[4]

Personal:	How are you?
Interpersonal:	Is there anything between us?
Task:	What's the work?

Check-Outs

Check-outs are also ignited with a brief CS that names the purpose of the check-out and poses an EQ that acknowledges the work of the group. This EQ also transitions the group to next steps and action.

A standard check-out that you can use in many types of meetings allows people to quickly transition from the work of the meeting to the action after the meeting. It is a series of three Effective PIT Questions:

Personal:	How are you right now?
Interpersonal:	What do you appreciate about the work of the group?
Task:	What is your next step or commitment to action?

APPLICATION:
CONNECTS GROUP TO EACH OTHER AND THE MEETING RESULTS
THROUGH CHECK-IN AND CHECK-OUT

You are applying this skill when:

- *you consider the relationships of the people to each other and the work in framing the check-in and check-out.*

- *you use check-ins and check-outs that illuminate B/ART and make it more likely that members will contribute their resources to the meeting result.*

- *you use check-outs that address whether meeting results were achieved and elicit how group members felt about the meeting experience.*

Check-In Questions

Here are some examples of check-in questions that join people to each other (personal and interpersonal) and to the work (results):

Relationship-connections questions (personal and interpersonal)

- How are you today?
- What name do you prefer that people call you?
- What values do you bring to this work?
- Who are three people who inspire you in your work?

Resource questions

- What talent or asset do you bring to this group?
- What is your learning style?
- What is one thing that, if people knew it, could help them work well with you?

Meeting-result-connections questions

- What would you like to accomplish in this meeting?
- What would make the time you spend here worthwhile?
- What would you like to walk away with from the meeting?
- If this meeting is successful, what will you have?
  What will you be able to do?
- What do you not want to have happen at this meeting?

Check-Out Questions

Here are some examples of check-out questions that mirror the structure of the check-in questions.

Relationship-connections questions (personal and interpersonal)

- In a word or short phrase, how you are right now?
- What have you appreciated about the time spent together?

Resource questions

- What will you take away from this meeting to your daily work?
- What knowledge, insight, or wisdom have you gained from the meeting?
- What will you do differently based on the work here today?
- What worked? Didn't work? What would you have done differently?

Meeting-result-connections questions

- On a scale of one to ten, how would you rate the progress toward the meeting results?
- Rate progress on each meeting result: high, medium, or low.
- What is your next step? What is one commitment you can make?

MASTERY:
READS GROUP TO INFORM CHECK-IN AND CHECK-OUT

You are demonstrating mastery of this skill when:

- *you use the technique of checking in and out flexibly during a series of conversations or to facilitate transitions from one meeting result to another.*

- *you use check-in or check-out to explore hypotheses about group dynamics or make the group aware of group dynamics.*

- *you use check-ins and check-outs at the beginning and end of meetings and the beginning and end of conversations to move a group to action.*

The choice of check-in and check-out questions is limited only by your imagination and experience. Here are some examples:

- Ask people to say how they are doing at the Person-Role-System level and provide a context for the group to see possibilities for aligned action within B/ART.

- In groups that are familiar with MBTI, have people share something about their MBTI preferences to highlight differential impact, the phenomena that the same experience will affect people in different ways.

- Emphasize accountability and ask people to share their progress in keeping their commitments since the last meeting.

Similarly, a check-out might do the following:

- Ask people to say how they feel about the experience and briefly state a next step or commitment to action.

- Highlight differential impact by inviting people to say what they have learned about the similarities and differences in the group and what they will take back home to work better together.

- Emphasize accountability and ask people to make one offer to a group member and one request of support from a member to keep their commitment to action.

TIPS: CHECKING IN AND CHECKING OUT

DO

- Align the check-in with the meeting purpose and results. As the adage goes, well begun is half done, so be intentional with your EQs.

- Use check-in and check-out during the course of a meeting to transition from conversation to conversation or to mark transitions from one part of the meeting (e.g., morning to lunch) to another.

- Use check-in and check-out to make mood and emotion apparent to the group.

- Use a check-out to see if the group is ready to move on. After the check-out, ask: "Is the group ready to move on?"

- Use check-out questions to encourage explicit accountability for action (e.g., each person says what he or she will do when) and probe for a specific date or time.

- Use check-in to illuminate what the group is ready to do. Encourage listening and include a brief synthesis of the check-in as a transition to the work.

- Use the check-in to establish your relationship (B/ART) with the group by explicitly stating your role and your result.

DON'T

- Don't waste precious time at the beginning with work that is diversionary or not purposeful. For example, don't play games unless they connect people to the work.

- Don't ignore beginnings and endings of conversations and work during the day.

- Don't ignore how people are feeling, how they feel about each other, or how they feel about the work.

- Don't assume that the group is ready to move to the next step or next conversation.

- Don't ignore that accountable action always has a "when."

- Don't forget that the audience for the check-in is the group members.

- Don't forget that the check-in provides an opportunity for you to join with the group in role.

PARTICIPANT PRACTICE GUIDE 3.5:
CHECK IN AND CHECK OUT

Conversations often seem to have no clear beginning and peter out with no discernible conclusion or progress. The skill of checking in and checking out contributes to meetings beginning with a clarity of purpose and concluding with a sense of accomplishment. This guide offers suggestions on how to use check-ins and check-outs in your daily work.

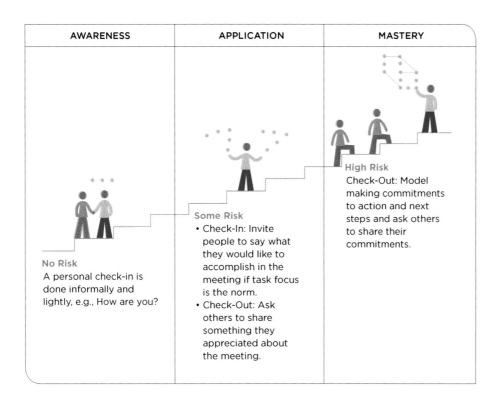

NOTES:

[1] Use references such as the book *Flip Charts: How to Draw Them and How Use Them* by Richard C. Brandt to learn more about tools and techniques.

[2] Brock. *Using Type in Selling: Building Relationships with the Myers-Briggs Type Indicator.* Consulting Psychologists Press. 1994.

[3] Gardner. *Five Minds of the Future.* Harvard Business Press Books. 2009.

[4] Bob Hoffman contributed the PIT check-in during the development of the *Resident Leadership and Facilitation Workbook*.

HOLD 3R MEETINGS

DEFINITION: USE THE 3R FRAMEWORK TO DESIGN AND FACILITATE MEETINGS THAT MOVE GROUPS FROM TALK TO ACTION

> THE MEETING RESULTS ARE THE PROMISE; THE AGENDA IS THE POSSIBILITY.
>
> –VICTORIA GODDARD-TRUITT

CONCEPTS IN THIS CHAPTER

THE 3Rs: RELATIONSHIPS, RESOURCES, AND RESULTS

APPLYING THE 3R FRAMEWORK

SKILLS FOR THIS COMPETENCY

4.1 USE THE 3Rs TO DESIGN THE MEETING

4.2 USE THE 3Rs IN THE MEETING TO ACHIEVE RESULTS

The 3Rs — Relationships, Resources, and Results — are essential tools for effective meetings. In this chapter, you'll learn how to hold 3R meetings that are both planned in advance and responsive to the needs of the group in the moment.

》 **Meeting result:** a step that produces action toward program, community, or population results

relationships

$+$ resources

$=$ results

THE 3Rs: RELATIONSHIPS, RESOURCES, AND RESULTS

Mental models articulate the how and why of the way people do work or the way people could work. RBF's underlying mental model for designing and executing meetings posits that people who are in relationship with each other and are focused on a common result can work to use their resources (talent, expertise, influence, authority, money, access, goods, services, property) to take action together.

The 3R framework is a mental model that is applied in the design and execution of meetings. 3R meetings are designed and implemented so that people's relationships plus the resources they bring to the work will add up to results.

APPLYING THE 3R FRAMEWORK

In meetings, the 3Rs are used to formulate Context Statements, Effective Questions, and Listen Fors to frame conversations. The framework is also used to design meetings. In meeting design, the framework represents a thinking process that can be used by a participant, convener, or facilitator to prepare for a meeting, and/or as an interactive co-design process in which the convener, facilitator, and/or some or all of the participants work together to develop:

- *the common result that can bring people together.*
- *an understanding of how the participants relate to each other and how they relate to the common result.*
- *the resources that the participants have or have access to that could contribute to the result.*

In the meeting design process or conversation, exploration can start with any of the 3Rs (relationships, resources, or results); however, it is important to touch on all three. The 3R meeting design is an iterative process in which insights emerge along the way that shape the desired meeting results, the choice of appropriate participants, and the preparation needed for accomplishing the meeting results.

Using the 3R mental model in the two ways described above creates a parallel structure from the level of conversations to the level of whole meetings. This parallel structure allows 3R meetings to be both intentional — prepared for in advance — and responsive and adaptive in the meeting itself. For example, if the group needs more or less time to discuss a topic or discovers new issues to discuss, the agenda is adapted to be responsive to the work the group is doing and needs to do to accomplish the meeting results. The use of the 3R framework during the meeting supports the responsive adaptation of the agenda by enabling the group to attend to relationship and resources as they make decisions about what they want to do, how they want to do it, and how what they are doing will support them in accomplishing the desired meeting results.

SKILLS FOR THIS COMPETENCY

SKILL 4.1: USE THE 3Rs TO DESIGN THE MEETING

The table below defines and describes the skill of using the 3Rs to design meetings. Use the questions to assess your current skill level and focus your practice and develop mastery in the use of the skill.

AWARENESS	APPLICATION	MASTERY
Understands the interrelationship and use of the 3Rs as they relate to the design of a meeting agenda • Do I clearly articulate the results for meetings (specific, observable, measurable)? • Do the proposed meeting results contribute to a program or organizational result?	Uses EQs and LFs to elicit what the group wants to accomplish, who is and needs to be involved, and what people have and can bring to achieve the desired results • Do I use B/ART in analyzing the composition of groups to explore who might be invited to contribute to meeting results? • Do I assess if those invited can accomplish the meeting results with their relationships and resources?	Designs the meeting agenda and environment for the group to own its work by applying the 3Rs • Do I align meeting preparation and design with the desired results? • Do I ensure that the required resources are accessible at the meeting? • Do I recognize and encourage people aligning their resources to achieve results?

AWARENESS:
UNDERSTANDS THE INTERRELATIONSHIP AND USE OF THE 3Rs AS THEY RELATE TO THE DESIGN OF A MEETING AGENDA

You are aware of this skill when:

• *you can clearly articulate the results for meetings (specific, observable, measurable).*

• *you see the proposed meeting results contribute to a program or organizational result.*

What Are Meeting Results?

In developing the 3R competency, the first step is to have a clear understanding of what meetings results are and to have a method for developing and articulating them. Meeting results are:

- produced when the work of the participants in a meeting is successful.

- the product of constructive, focused conversations (i.e., conversation results produce meeting results).

- specific, observable, and measurable; you can tell whether the results occurred or not.

- varied by the type of work being done and the capacity of the group to address issues and move to action.

- cumulative and build toward accomplishing the meeting purpose.

- connected to a meeting purpose that is a step along the way to the program, organizational, or community results.

The Meeting Results Guide on the next page defines 12 meeting results typical of the work groups do to move from talk to action. For each of the 12 types of results, there are three examples of how to articulate that result along a continuum of low to high impact. A high-impact meeting result is one that is almost certain to help the group move to action. Strive to articulate meeting results that are as high impact as possible. Keep in mind that the low- and medium-impact results can be valuable when used as building blocks to the achievement of high-impact meeting results.

Using the Meeting Results Guide

Collaborative work occurs when people come together and get things done — with focus on a common purpose and an orientation to action. Having productive meetings with clear results that lead to action enhances collaborative work.

Meetings are more effective when people come to the meeting with the results the meeting is intended to accomplish in mind. In the context of the collaborative work cycle, entering with meeting results in mind makes it more probable that people will move to action and make commitments.

As a participant, convener, or meeting facilitator, you can use the Meeting Results Guide to inform your preparation and have more productive meetings by coming with meeting results in mind and leaving with action commitments in hand. Use this guide to articulate the meeting purpose and the meeting results. Use the blank rows to fill in meeting results not covered.

MEETING RESULTS GUIDE

TYPE OF MEETING RESULT	LOW IMPACT	MEDIUM IMPACT	HIGH IMPACT
Ready to work together Establish a foundation of an agreed-upon set of results that are important to the participants and confirm that the participants are committed to each other and their task.	Know each other's names and roles.	Reach mutual agreement on results and identify each person's interest in the group and its work.	Understand how the roles, authority, and resources each person brings will contribute to achieving mutually agreed-upon results.
Relationships strengthened Foster active participation, open communication, and effective collaboration.	Agree on norms related to working well together.	Hold each other accountable for adhering to norms.	Candidly explore differing perspectives and confidently address difficult/sensitive issues.
Information shared Transfer knowledge to advance the work.	Provide status reports or educational presentations.	Discuss potential relevance of knowledge transfer for the work.	Identify implications from knowledge transfer and use to advance the work.
Ideas generated Brainstorm and explore possibilities.	List new ideas.	Identify which new ideas to explore.	Prioritize new ideas using agreed-upon criteria.
Problem solved Overcome obstacles to advance the work.	Identify causes and brainstorm ideas to address them.	Evaluate ideas and develop robust recommendations for solving problems.	Make commitments to implement selected solutions.
Feedback/input secured Gather information to improve the work.	Share feedback and/or improvement suggestions.	Explore feedback and identify implications for work.	Agree on revisions to work in response to feedback.
Strategy/Action Plan developed Decide what to do to achieve results.	Identify potential activities.	Define desired destination and key steps to get there.	Sequence and schedule actions, identifying any critical path dependencies.
Decisions made Make choices together about what to do.	Make a decision.	Each person commits to support the decision.	Hold each other accountable for implementing the decision.
Conflict resolved Address dynamics that inhibit progress.	Acknowledge and describe conflict.	Identify and explore sources of conflict.	Commit to actions to resolve conflict.
Accountability strengthened Publicly report progress on commitments.	Report progress on commitments.	Report progress and identify areas needing improvement.	Report progress and problem solve how to either get back on track or sustain momentum.
Progress recognized Acknowledge what has been accomplished.	Review milestones.	Celebrate progress or admit lack of progress on milestones.	Include key stakeholders in celebration or postmortem.
Commitments to action made Publicly say who will do what by when.	Say who will do what.	Say who will do what by when.	Say who will do what by when and set quality expectations.

Select the Meeting Results

After defining purpose, review the Meeting Results Guide to select the meeting results that will move the group toward achieving the meeting purpose. Use the Meeting Results Guide to help you articulate the results selected in a way that is more likely to move the group to action. If the results you are looking for are not listed in the guide, use examples in the guide to inform how you articulate the additional meeting results.

When you select meeting results, always include the first meeting result (ready to work together) to begin meetings, and the last result (commitments to action made) for the end of meetings. Including these two results ensures that you will come with meeting results in mind and leave with action commitments in hand. Often the check-in is designed to achieve the "ready to work together" meeting result and the check-out is designed to achieve the "commitments to action made" meeting result.

Meeting result statements should have the following qualities:

- *Be clear and specific:* Can I describe the desired result so others will understand?

- *Be observable:* Will I be able to tell if the result happened or not?

- *Be meaningful:* Will accomplishing this result make important and valuable progress toward our ultimate goals for the work?

- *Be feasible:* Do I honestly believe we can achieve this result?
  Do we have sufficient influence and/or resources to achieve this result?

The Meeting Results Guide provides examples of meeting results along a continuum from low impact to high impact. The examples may stretch you to formulate more impactful meeting results or to see how achieving a lower-impact meeting result can be a step along the way to achieving a higher-impact meeting. Once your meeting results are clear, you can sequence them and include them in an agenda.

APPLICATION: USES EQs AND LFs TO ELICIT WHAT THE GROUP WANTS TO ACCOMPLISH, WHO IS AND NEEDS TO BE INVOLVED, AND WHAT PEOPLE HAVE AND CAN BRING TO ACHIEVE THE DESIRED RESULTS

You are applying the this skill when:

- *you use B/ART when analyzing the composition of groups to explore who might be invited to contribute to meeting results.*

- *you assess if those invited can accomplish the meeting results through their relationships and resources.*

The awareness of the range of meeting results and how those results contribute to organizational and program results can be used within the 3R framework to design meetings.

As a reminder, the 3R framework is:

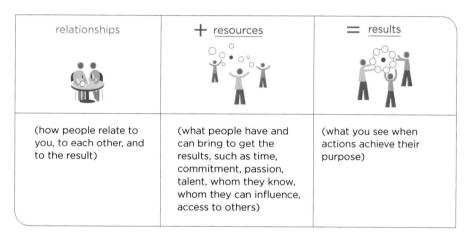

relationships	+ resources	= results
(how people relate to you, to each other, and to the result)	(what people have and can bring to get the results, such as time, commitment, passion, talent, whom they know, whom they can influence, access to others)	(what you see when actions achieve their purpose)

Effective Questions (EQs) for Meeting Design

Meetings that produce results sometimes happen by accident, but results are more likely to occur if prepared for by design. The 3R design process is a series of EQs that, when answered in an integrated manner, lay the foundation for a meeting that is more likely to move from talk to action.

The 3R design process, though iterative, often begins with an idea about the purpose of the meeting and some preliminary results. You can use the EQs listed in the following sections to help generate a 3R meeting design.

MEETING PURPOSE EQs

- What would it look like if this meeting were successful?

- If a miracle happened, what would you accomplish here today?

- What do you need to do to make this meeting valuable to you?

> Get new information?
  – What type of information?
  – From whom?

> Solve problems?
  – What kind of problems? Relationship problems?
  – Strategy problems?

> Make decisions?
  – What kind of decisions?
  – Whom will they affect and what difference will they make?

Answering these questions informs your understanding of a meeting's purpose, which can then be expressed in a brief statement. The meeting results add up to or accomplish the meeting purpose.

RESULTS EQs

When defining the meeting results, a few overarching questions may be helpful:

- What needs to be accomplished during the meeting to achieve the meeting purpose?

- What do we want to have at the end of the meeting and how will we get there?

- How would you measure progress?

Answers to the overarching questions need to be filtered through the lens of the other two Rs in the 3R framework. That is, a successful meeting aligns the relationships and resources of those invited with the meeting results. When considering relationships and resources, the following questions may be helpful:

RELATIONSHIPS EQs

- Who will come to the meeting? or Who might come to the meeting?

- What is their relationship to the meeting results?

- Are they neutral, uninformed, or strongly for or against the meeting results?

- Do they care about the meeting results? Why?

- What is their role in relationship to the meeting results, e.g., what is the boundary of their authority related to the work of the meeting?

- Do they have formal authority in relationship to the people or tasks associated with the result?

- Do they have informal authority in relationship to the people or tasks associated with the meeting results?

- To whom are they accountable for any of the tasks associated with the meeting results? For the meeting results as a whole? For the program or organizational work that the meeting results contribute to?

- What are their relationships to each other?

- Do they know each other? How well do they know each other?

- In the context of this meeting, are they peers, friends, competitors, neighbors, partners, boss/employees, provider/customers, etc.?

- In the context of other relationships they may have, are they peers, friends, competitors, neighbors, partners, boss/employees, provider/customers, etc.?

RESOURCES EQs

- What do the people coming to the meeting already have or know that can contribute to the meeting results?

- What are the MBTIs of the people coming? How can those preferences contribute to accomplishing the meeting results?

- What are the backgrounds, experiences, genders, races, ethnicities, languages, professional areas of expertise, and ages of the people coming to the meeting? How can these characteristics contribute to accomplishing the meeting results?

- What do people need to know before or during the meeting to accomplish the results?

- What is the time available for the meeting?

- Where is the meeting?

- How can the space be used to support the meeting result?

The answers to the 3R EQs above help you design and execute a meeting with the results, commitments, and next steps needed to move to action.

Listen Fors (LFs) for Meeting Design

When used in conjunction with EQs, the Listen Fors for each of the 3Rs contribute to developing 3R designs. The intentional use of the LFs enables information about any of the 3Rs to be heard and captured whenever that information is offered. Listening for all 3Rs simultaneously is an opportunity to practice charting multiple categories for later synthesis.

RESULTS LFS

- People's pictures of success, such as the result that the meeting result could lead to. Examples might include, more youth staying in school and doing well academically.

- Decisions made, problems solved, good feelings about each other and the work.

- The benefits of actions, such as more youth in mentoring programs or the number of mentors recruited.

- The quality of actions, such as the percentage of mentors who spend five hours a week with their mentee.

RELATIONSHIPS LFS

- Names and affiliations of those invited or to be invited.

- Missing people or organizations that might contribute to the result.

- Influencers who can reach out to potential participants or authorize their participation.

RESOURCES LFs

- What people can do.

- Whom people know.

- Whom people can influence.

- What people care about.

- What conveners or others can do to help those invited be active, engaged participants.

- Preparation requests for participants that will support their engagement.

Composition Analysis

Composition analysis provides information about the group — who is or will be at the meeting. This information helps you consider what work the group can do together that falls within each individual's and the group's role, authority (formal or informal), and daily work. In addition, composition analysis reveals the Person-Role-System dynamics in the group and informs meeting design by highlighting the resources that people bring to the work and the relationships that support achieving results.[1]

An initial composition analysis in the design phase is useful to identify gaps in roles and/or organizations of those invited. Revisiting the analysis after the design has matured can identify possible table grouping and/or potential friction points between people or productive pairings. The table on the next page suggests a format for a thorough composition analysis.

SAMPLE COMPOSITION ANALYSIS

RELATIONSHIPS		RESULTS		RESOURCES
Person		Role	System	Influence, Impact, Leverage
Name and characteristics *MBTI, age, gender, race, ethnicity, language*	**Professional background** *Area of study, experience*	**Title/role** *Authority regarding task related to meeting results or people attending the meeting*	**Organization and sector** *Accountability: to whom and for what*	**For each participant, consider** • *Whom can the participant influence formally and informally* • *What does the participant have direct control over* • *What can the participant do through connections and relationships* • *What are the participant's passion, values, commitment, knowledge*

Often these data are not available before the meeting and are generated during the meeting. However, gathering even some of the data and using that information during the design process aligns the design with the most important elements of meeting success — the people in the meeting. The investment of time in and attention to a thorough composition analysis is a practical way to ensure sufficient focus is put on who the people are, what they might want for themselves, and how they might contribute to the meeting results. The composition analysis then informs the design and hypotheses about potential group dynamics.

Meeting Results by Design

3R meeting results consist of problems solved, relationships built, knowledge shared, opportunities identified and explored, decisions made, and commitments to take action. If, by the end of a meeting, there is no clarity or documentation of key decisions, no commitments to action, and no immediate next steps, then the meeting will not likely lead to improved conditions.

The table on the next page illustrates examples of RBF skills and meeting preparation for several types of meeting results and activities.

MEETING RESULT	TYPE OF ACTIVITY OR CONVERSATION	RBF SKILL OR PROCESS	PREPARATION
Relationships strengthened	People getting to know each other	• Use relationship check-in • Use group norms • Eat together	• Gather materials • Bring food, stress toys
Information shared	People learning new things	• Storytelling • Reviewing highlights of a report • Coaching/feedback	• Choose topic • Prepare report • Read report • Ask reflective practice EQs
Ideas generated	Creative thinking	• Use Post-It notes • Draw pictures • Set context, EQs	• Gather materials for affinity grouping exercises and brainstorming
Issues explored	Inquiry and dialogue	• Use paired conversation • Set context, EQs	• Background or briefing papers reviewed • Analysis of issues from different perspectives
Solutions developed	Problem solving	• Define problems • Create options • Set context, EQs	• Pairings to enhance mutual understanding • Background reading on promising practices • Examples of what is working
Decisions made	Making choices together	• Proposal-based decision making • Set context, EQs	• Summary of survey findings of people's preferred solutions • Reflective practice EQs to identify sources of conflict
Commitments made	Negotiating requests/contributions	• Dialogue to identify barriers to action and what is needed to overcome them • Set context, EQs	• Action commitment forms (two-part carbonless forms). The meeting convener keeps the top page for group documentation and accountability, and the participant keeps the second page as his or her copy to ensure follow through on the commitment. • Template for documentation of commitments

Effective design requires information gathering, analysis/diagnosis, considering options, choosing an approach, and refining the approach — before, during, and after the meeting. One approach is to design the meeting backward from the meeting results. First, consider the results you want to achieve by the end of the meeting. Think backward from these results by asking yourself, "If we accomplished that result, what would we have been doing just before it was accomplished?" In considering what types of conversations produce different types of results, think about how the facilitator uses the RBF skills to help the group achieve results. For each meeting result, consider what preparation is required.

MASTERY:

DESIGNS THE MEETING AGENDA AND ENVIRONMENT FOR GROUP TO OWN THEIR WORK BY APPLYING THE 3Rs

You are demonstrating mastery of this skill when:

- *you align meeting preparation and design with desired results.*

- *you ensure that the required resources are accessible at the meeting.*

- *you recognize and encourage resource alignment at the meeting.*

The meeting environment is often something you cannot control. The table below highlights some of the ideal aspects and the alternatives in case you cannot get the ideal. The ideal meeting includes a team of convener, facilitator, co-facilitator, and documenter.

IDEAL AND NON-IDEAL SETTINGS[2]

IDEAL SETTING	NON-IDEAL SETTING
• Windows/natural light	• Use natural or artificial plants/flowers or lamps.
• Bright (but not harsh) light	• Use table lamps and colored paper as filters.
• Clear lines of sight (no columns in the middle of the room)	• Arrange tables around columns and use columns to post information.
• Quiet and controllable heating and air conditioning systems	• Acknowledge the discomfort and make paper fans, share sweaters, etc. • Acknowledge the strain and ask people to speak louder and use microphones.
• Enough room so people can sit comfortably at their tables and pull back a bit for two- and three-person conversations. Space for people to walk around.	• Acknowledge discomfort and thank people for their patience; use more frequent stretch breaks or ways to get people moving or standing.
• Walls you can use to post flip chart pages	• Provide additional flip chart stands.
• Nearby restrooms with enough capacity for both men and women	• Take more frequent and longer breaks.
• Cellular reception and, if possible, a wireless connection	• Take longer breaks for people to find cellular reception. Provide memory sticks for recorders.
• Laptops for the meeting documenter and a laptop on each table for table recorders. Printer and access to copying. LCD display.	• Have forms available to document strategies and action plans. Access to a business office with a printer and copier.
• A square-shaped room to accommodate people sitting at tables in a half circle, with flip charts at the front of the room. Options: » Round or half-round tables set with four to seven chairs (don't allow chairs with backs to block the front of the room). » Rectangular tables with chairs on three sides forming the spines of a fan shape. » An open U with flip charts in the front. » For small groups, people seated around three sides of a table with the flip chart in front.	• Work within limitations of the room to create the best approximation you can of the half circle. For example: SUPPORT / DOCUMENTER FLIP CHART FACILITATOR FLIP CHART

Public and Annotated Agendas

Everyone is familiar with public meeting agendas that include the meeting title, date, time, and location. The public agenda often has the times and a brief title of each activity or discussion. An RBF public agenda has all this information plus the meeting purpose and results. The agenda ensures that for each conversation enough information is provided to move through the conversation and accomplish the meeting results.

The annotated agenda acts as a playbook for the team implementing the meeting. This team might be only the facilitator and the convener or a group of four or five people with the additional roles of co-facilitator for charting, documenter for capturing decisions and action commitments, and — for large, complex meetings — a site captain to manage logistics (discussed in Book Two).

With more complex meetings, the annotated agenda adds guidance for in room set-up, transitions, and materials or actions needed to achieve the results. The exercise below provides an example of how to develop an annotated agenda.

Once the annotated agenda is developed, the public agenda may be produced by simply deleting the "Notes" column and the detailed outline of the conversations, leaving only the time, segment title, and the result for each meeting segment.

PRACTICE: PREPARING AN ANNOTATED AGENDA

Think of an upcoming meeting in which you, as a participant, convener, or facilitator, can have a role in shaping the meeting's purpose, results, and design. This meeting design exercise has three parts.

PART #1: GATHER 3Rs INFORMATION

Meeting Purpose and Results
- What is the meeting's purpose?
- Whose purpose is it?
- What meeting results do you want to achieve?
- What work does this group need to do to accomplish the results?

Relationships and Resources
- Who are the participants? What are their relationships to each other and to the meeting's purpose? Use the composition analysis format to document this information.
- How many people need to attend to achieve the results?
- Who can contribute and how in order to achieve the purpose?

Logistics
- How much time is available?
- Where is the meeting location?
- What preparation is needed to enable people to do the work in the time and space available?

PART #2: IDENTIFY THE WORK AND DESIGN

As you consider what you know about the people, purpose, and results, answer the following questions about your meeting results. Take the opportunity to work backward from the last meeting result.

Identify the sequence of the work of the meeting and formulate the design or process for how the work can occur for each result.

What Are the Desired Meeting Results?
• What is the work or activity that will accomplish this result?
• What kind of conversation will support the work or activity?
• How much time will it take to achieve the results?
• What will each person have or what will the group have if the meeting is successful? That is, what results transition the work of the meeting to next steps and action?

PART #3: TRANSLATE THE WORK OF THE MEETING INTO AN ANNOTATED AGENDA

Parts 1 and 2 of this exercise are used to complete the annotated agenda template (below). For each meeting result, set a beginning and end time, and name the meeting segment (topic). Identify the Context Statement and EQ that can begin the work for that topic in the Task/Result column. To ensure that you are working backward from the result, go to the next to last row (indicated by the arrow) of the template and fill in the meeting result. Then sequence the meeting results back to the beginning of the meeting.

In the Notes column, specify the physical setup of the room and list what is needed in terms of materials or processes to successfully accomplish the work and have the conversations for each result.

3Rs ANNOTATED AGENDA TEMPLATE

Title

Type of Meeting

When

Where

Meeting Purpose:

Meeting Results: *By the end of the meeting, the participants will have:*

• _____

• _____

• _____

Participants:

Preparation:

SAMPLE AGENDA

TIME	TASK/RESULT	NOTES
Start	**Topic: Welcome and Purpose (Check-in)** *1. Convener welcomes people, highlights purpose and results and introduces facilitator.* *2. Facilitator EQs for check-in:* *• How are you this morning?* *• What result do you want from today's meeting?* *3. Facilitator synthesis of check-in and whole group discussion to modify agenda if needed.* **Meeting Result:** *People are ready to work together.*	Room setup: table, chairs, flip chart stands, AV, materials, refreshments, breaks and meals [3]
	Topic: TBD **Meeting Result:**	Facilitator charts discussion and decisions.
	Topic: TBD **Meeting Result:**	Facilitator charts discussion and decisions
	Topic: Next Steps (Check-out) *1. Facilitator sets context for check-out based on work accomplished during the meeting and uses the following EQs:* *• What progress did you make toward your meeting result?* *• What will you do by when to build on the work of this meeting?* *2. Facilitator Listens For and records specifically what each person will do by when to accurately capture action commitments.* *3. Convener makes closing remarks expressing appreciation for the group's work, convener's own commitments to action, and reminds people that decisions and action commitments from the meeting will be posted electronically by close of business the next day.* **Meeting Result:** *People commit to who will do what when to move forward together.*	Facilitator chart of action commitments to be transcribed and posted electronically by close of business the next day.
End	***Adjourn***	

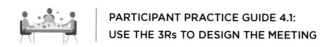

PARTICIPANT PRACTICE GUIDE 4.1:
USE THE 3Rs TO DESIGN THE MEETING

3R meetings predictably move groups from talk to action. However, most meetings are not prepared for or executed using the 3R framework. This Participant Practice Guide describes approaches that participants can use to apply the 3R framework to make the meetings they attend more productive.

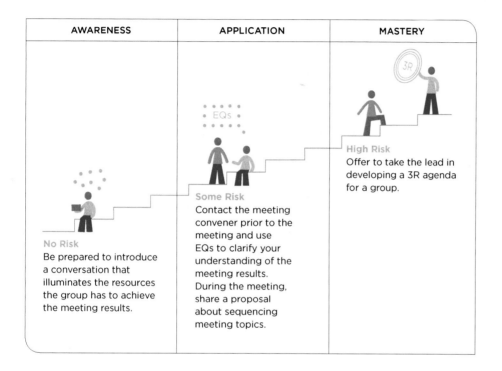

AWARENESS	APPLICATION	MASTERY
No Risk Be prepared to introduce a conversation that illuminates the resources the group has to achieve the meeting results.	**Some Risk** Contact the meeting convener prior to the meeting and use EQs to clarify your understanding of the meeting results. During the meeting, share a proposal about sequencing meeting topics.	**High Risk** Offer to take the lead in developing a 3R agenda for a group.

SKILL 4.2: USE THE 3Rs IN THE MEETING TO ACHIEVE RESULTS

The table below defines and describes the skill at three levels of development. Answering the questions assesses your current level of skill and provides a focus for ongoing practice.

AWARENESS	APPLICATION	MASTERY
Understands the inter-relationships and use of the 3Rs to help groups achieve results • *Do the meeting results align with the meeting purpose?* • *Do all meeting results add up to the purpose?*	Uses EQs and LFs with the group to elicit 3Rs during the meeting • *Do the CS, EQs, and LFs achieve the meeting result?*	Creates an environment for the group to own its work by applying the 3Rs. Captures decisions, commitments, etc., in a 3R framework • *Do I use the 3R framework to follow up on meetings to move from talk to action?* • *Do I capture decisions and commitments in terms of who will do what when, how, and with whom, and with what resources?*

AWARENESS:
UNDERSTANDS THE INTERRELATIONSHIPS AND USE OF THE 3Rs TO HELP GROUPS ACHIEVE RESULTS

You are aware of this skill when:

• *you align meeting results with the meeting purpose.*

• *you see that all the meeting results add up to the purpose.*

Meeting Preparation

Preparation is an important aspect of effective meetings. If participants are unprepared or underprepared, critical time can be wasted. However, demanding an excessive level of pre-work or overpreparation can also set a barrier between the participants and the results. The following are examples of what can be provided before meetings to help participants prepare:

• Effective Questions

• Targeted readings

• Handouts

• Relationship building/interviews

• Information about the where and when of the meeting

As part of meeting preparation, consider who will play what roles. The possible roles include convener, facilitator, co-facilitator, participants, or others who can inform the meeting design (co-designers), and people who can handle on-site logistics.

The following questions enable people to prepare for, conduct, and follow up on meetings.

BEFORE THE MEETING

- Who will attend the meeting?

- When, how, and who will invite them?

- Do any participants have special needs? Do new members need someone to orient them to the work of the group?

- Who is the facilitator? The co-facilitator?

- Is there a chair or other authority figure? What is his or her relationship to the facilitator?

- Who will write/type the notes?

- Who will bring the materials?

- Who will participate in designing the meeting?

- Who will make decisions about the content of the agenda?

- Who will present issues or proposals? Do they have the information they need?

- Who will handle logistics and answer the following questions:

  - Where will the meeting be held? Who is the contact person at the facility?

  - What is the day and time of the meeting? How long will it run?

  - What arrangements are needed for transportation, child care, and meals?

  - What materials, media, or supplies are needed?

  - Should refreshments be available?

  - How will the room be set up?

  - Who will handle the room setup on the day of the meeting?

AFTER THE MEETING

- Who will distribute the notes?

- Who will be involved in debriefing the meeting?

- Who will send out a short summary of decisions at the meeting and key actions to take (including who and when)?

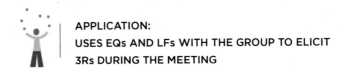

APPLICATION:
USES EQs AND LFs WITH THE GROUP TO ELICIT
3Rs DURING THE MEETING

You are applying this skill when:

• *you see the CS, EQs, and LFs achieve the meeting result.*

Design Conversations

Once you have sequenced the meeting results and identified processes for the work and materials, the next step is to give more thought to the conversations that will support the work. Follow the steps below to practice designing a conversation for one meeting result by developing an initial Context Statement, Effective Question, and Listen For.

GETTING READY

- Select one meeting result from your annotated agenda and identify an issue that will need discussion.
- Identify the conversation result that is a step toward the overall meeting result.
- Develop a CS, EQ, and LF to initiate the conversation.

PRACTICE

- Place the CS on the top of a flip chart.
- Use the initial EQ and LF to begin the conversation.
- Facilitate the conversation with colleagues who can provide feedback, using SBI, on your use of skills.
- Assess the effectiveness of your CS, EQ, and LF in framing a conversation.

MASTERY: CREATES AN ENVIRONMENT FOR THE GROUP TO OWN THEIR WORK BY APPLYING THE 3Rs. CAPTURES DECISIONS, COMMITMENTS, ETC., IN A 3R FRAMEWORK

You are demonstrating mastery of this skill when:

- *you use the 3R framework to design, prepare for, implement, and follow up on meetings to move groups from talk to action.*

- *you capture decisions and commitments in terms of who will do what when, how, with whom, and with what resources.*

Productive meetings are most likely when all aspects of meeting preparation, execution, and follow-up are kept in mind. Meetings that involve participants from more than one organization are more complex and benefit from a structured process to develop and prepare for the meeting. The following resources outline a more formal, structured process for use in preparation, execution, and follow-up for more complex meetings:

- 3Rs Checklist

- 3Rs Annotated Agenda Templates and Flip Chart Documentation

Less complex meetings may not need as much structure or formal preparation. When a more informal process is appropriate, the All-in-One Agenda template later in this chapter is a resource that simplifies preparation and follow-up by integrating the agenda and the documentation of action commitments into one document.

The 3Rs Checklist on the next page enables participants to enter with meeting results in mind and leave the meeting with commitments to action in hand.

3Rs CHECKLIST

STEP	ACTION	DETAILED STEPS
1	**Results focus**	Use the skills of hold role, appreciative openness, B/ART, and 3Rs to bring a results focus to the work. Take time to do the following: • Know what the meeting is about. • Understand why the meeting is taking place. • Understand the participants' expectations. • Know what the participants really want out of the meeting. • Clarify and clearly state the meeting results(s) so that they are observable and actionable.
2	**3Rs preparation**	Prepare by developing a public agenda, annotated agenda, and composition analysis that accomplish the following: • They are grounded in a co-design process that explores people's connections, interests, and issues ahead of time (relationships). • They specify and make available the materials to be used before and during the meeting to inform the conversations (resources). • Communicate the meeting results to the participants in advance (results).
3	**3Rs facilitation**	In facilitating the meeting, use the competencies of hold roles, hold conversations, and hold groups to ensure the following: • Each person is heard. • Conversations focus on results. • The agenda is adapted as necessary to reflect the group's work. • The group makes decisions, identifies next steps, and commits to action.
4	**3Rs follow-up**	Support follow-up by ensuring that all group members: • have a common understanding of the decisions they have made. • follow through on actions after the meeting. • use information to support the group members' accountability for action commitments.

The annotated agenda templates and flip charts on the next few pages illustrate the use of the 3Rs method for a youth engagement program

A community multisector collaborative is committed to youth success in school and safety in the community (results). The Youth Engagement Subcommittee (YES) has implemented a late-night basketball program on the high school outdoor basketball courts. The program's purpose is to engage older youth, keep them safe, and connect them to youth counselors who encourage and support their success in school.

YES is convening a meeting with concerned neighbors who live next to the school and who are being disturbed by the noise of late-night basketball.

The subcommittee chair has invited one of the collaborative staff members to prepare for and facilitate the meeting. The facilitator prepared for the first meeting by having a co-design call with representatives of YES and the neighbors.

After the co-design call, the facilitator prepared and shared Annotated Agenda #1 with the co-designers and facilitated the first meeting. The results of the first meeting included actions, next steps, and a commitment to a second meeting with the collaborative board (see Flip Charts #1a and 1b).

The facilitator prepared and shared an agenda for the second meeting (Annotated Agenda #2) with the co-designers who provided feedback and suggestions. Meeting #2 built on solutions developed in Meeting #1 and, most important, the action commitments kept between Meeting #1 and #2.

The second meeting's results included decisions and actions resolving the neighbor's issues, continuing the program, and establishing an ongoing relationship between the program and the neighbors to continue to work together (see Flip Chart #2).

3R ANNOTATED AGENDA #1

Meeting Title: Youth Engagement Subcommittee Meeting #1

Type of Meeting: Problem-Solving Meeting

Purpose of Subcommittee Meeting: The Youth Engagement Subcommittee will develop solutions to address the neighbors' concerns about the noise caused by youth using the high school basketball court for late-night basketball.

Meeting Results: By the end of the subcommittee meeting, the participants will have:
• explored people's differing perceptions of the problem.
• identified who the parties to the problem are and explored their needs and fears.
• brainstormed solutions that could meet the different parties' needs and addressed their fears.
• chosen the solution(s) that shows the most promise in solving the problem.
• identified who will do what to make the solution(s) workable.
• committed to attend the Caring Community Board meeting to present the solution(s) for decision by the board.

Participants: Subcommittee members, youth program participants, and neighbors

Preparation:
• Give flyers to neighbors by going door-to-door, inviting them to the meeting, and asking them about their concerns.
• Post a sign on the basketball court announcing the meeting and inviting the youth.
• Give word-of-mouth invitation and flyers to youth, inviting their participation and asking them about their concerns.

YOUTH ENGAGEMENT SUBCOMMITTEE MEETING #1 AGENDA

TIME	TASK/RESULT	NOTES
7:30 pm	**Welcome and Purpose** 1. Subcommittee chair welcomes people and highlights purpose of the meeting. 2. Youth activities coordinator says what she wants from the meeting. 3. Neighbor who is also a member of the Caring Community Board says what she wants from the meeting. 4. Check-In: The chair asks each person to introduce himself/herself and say what he/she hopes to get out of the meeting. **Result: People are ready to work.**	• Chairs set up in a circle • Two flip charts, markers • Name tags • Table set up with markers and name tags, pizza, and soft drinks • Pencils, clip boards, and paper for participants
7:45 pm	**Defining People's Needs** 1. Using the solution chart (see below), ask each party to name what they need (probe to see what is most valued and what people care about and what they fear). The solution chart is a format to capture on a flip chart what different participants need from a solution. This information is used to determine the content of the solutions that satisfy people's needs. 2. Using the solution chart, explore the parties' significant fears or worries; don't dismiss what seem to be irrational fears; they are still motivating people. **Result: Identify which parties are affected by the problem and explore their needs and fears.**	• Solution chart on the flip chart • Parties: the immediate neighbors who dislike the noise, the neighbors who support the use of the court, the youth who use the court, and the youth activities coordinator who supports the use of the court
8:05 pm	**Developing Solutions** 1. In smaller groups, have people answer the question: What can each party do that might meet the other parties' needs and fears? 2. Poll the groups for their ideas for solutions. 3. Select the solutions that seem most workable to the larger group. **Result: People have chosen promising solutions.**	• Chart the pro/con for each solution on the solution implementation chart (see below) • Identify the next steps that need to be taken to move forward on defining what is needed to implement the solution
8:20 pm	**The Next Steps** 1. Find at least one volunteer for each workable solution to check out the solution prior to the board meeting and present the solution to board. 2. Invite everyone to the board meeting. 3. Thank all parties for their participation. **Result: People are committed to carrying forward the solutions.**	• Action commitments made to check out solutions before next meeting • The solution implementation chart documents who will do what by the next board meeting
8:30 pm	**Adjourn**	

FLIP CHART #1A (PROBLEM SOLVING): SOLUTION CHART: PEOPLE'S NEEDS

NEIGHBORS WHO SUPPORT LATE-NIGHT BASKETBALL	YOUTH COORDINATOR OF LATE-NIGHT BASKETBALL
Needs: • Place for their children or their neighbors' children to have safe activities at night • Less youth crime and vandalism *Fears:* • If court closes nothing else for youth to do • Immediate neighbors unsympathetic to youth needs and to the broader community needs	*Needs:* • Low-cost, popular activity to engage youth • Location for activity that is easy for youth to get to *Fears:* • Opposition to late-night basketball may damage support for other youth activities • Tensions between immediate neighbors and youth will lead to bad feelings
NEIGHBORS WHO DON'T SUPPORT LATE-NIGHT BASKETBALL	**YOUTH**
Needs: • Quiet at night to sleep • No trash on their yards *Fears:* • Youth vandalism	*Needs:* • Place to hang out *Fears:* • Adults hassling them

FLIP CHART #1B (PROBLEM SOLVING): SOLUTION IMPLEMENTATION CHART

SOLUTIONS	NEXT STEPS BEFORE BOARD MEETING	PROS	CONS	FOR WHOM
Find an indoor court	High school principal will identify an indoor court available for evening use.	• Provides safe activity • Eliminates noise	• Not as convenient • May cost money	• Youth coordinator • Neighbors • Immediate neighbors • Youth
Use outdoor court until 9 p.m. and then have alternate activity indoors	Youth coordinator and youth representative will develop a youth pledge and identify alternate indoor activities.	• Quiet for sleep	• Having to find an alternate activity	• Immediate neighbors • Youth • Youth coordinator
Rotate basketball among three neighborhood courts and use only on Fri. & Sat. nights between 7–11 p.m.	Parks and Recreation supervisor and youth representative will reserve neighborhood courts.	• Limits noise	• More difficult to manage • No activity most nights	• Neighbors • Youth coordinator • Youth

Type of Meeting: Decision-Making Collaborative Board Meeting

Purpose of Subcommittee Meeting: To make decision about future of late-night basketball program

Meeting Results: By the end of the board meeting, the board members will have:

• discussed the solutions presented by the subcommittee.

• made a decision as to which solution to implement.

• identified next steps to implement the decision.

Participants:

• Board members

• Youth Engagement Subcommittee chair and members

• Youth

• Neighbors

Preparation: Development of solutions by subcommittee:

• Announcement via email and fax to board members of special breakfast board meeting

• Calling to check availability of board members to ensure quorum for decision making

**YOUTH ENGAGEMENT SUBCOMMITTEE MEETING PRESENTATION
TO THE BOARD MEETING AGENDA**

TIME	TASK/RESULT	NOTES
7:30 am	**Welcome and Purpose** 1. Chair welcomes and highlights purpose of the meeting. 2. Check-In: Chair asks attendees to introduce themselves and say what they hope to get out of the meeting. **Result: People are ready to work.**	• Chairs and tables in a U for the board members; chairs for neighbors/youth • Two flip charts, markers, name plates, coffee
7:45 am	**Presentation of the Solutions** 1. Each of the people who volunteered to develop solutions presents his/her solution and highlights pros/cons and cost of implementation. **Result: Solutions are reviewed.**	• Chair flip charts solutions
8:05 am	**Making a Decision** 1. Chair entertains questions of clarification. 2. Using proposal-based decision making,* the board reaches consensus on one of the solutions. **Result: Decision is made.**	• Secretary records the decision
8:20 am	**Next Steps** 1. Decision made as to who needs to do what and when to implement solution. **Result: Identified next steps to implement decision.**	• Secretary records the next steps as captured on the decision and action commitment chart
8:25 am	**Closing Comments** 1. Check-Out: Each person says the one word that expresses his/her reaction to the meeting	
8:30 am	**Adjourn**	

*Proposal-based decision making is a method for reaching consensus, where proposals are made and then members of the group work together to craft a proposal that everyone can support. This method is more fully explained in *RBF Book Two: Advanced Skills.*

FLIP CHART #2 (SOLUTION IMPLEMENTATION): DECISION AND ACTION COMMITMENT CHART (RECORD OF BOARD DECISIONS AND NEXT STEPS)

DECISION	WHO	WHAT	WHEN	WITH WHOM
Youth use high school indoor court	High school principal	Make one in door court available from 8–10:30 p.m. every night for neighborhood youth	By Monday of next week	High school athletic director
Limit use of outdoor court to 8 p.m.	Neighborhood Association Chair	• Post signs re: 8 p.m. limit • Distribute leaflets to neighbors and youth • Station neighborhood and youth volunteers at outdoor court to support movement to indoor court at 8 p.m.	By next Friday	Neighborhood and youth volunteers to distribute flyers
Inform youth of new indoor and outdoor court use policy	Youth representatives and Parks and Recreation youth coordinator	Outreach to youth who use the outdoor court to inform them of availability of indoor court	By next Friday	• Youth coordinator • Youth

Integrating Preparation, Execution, and Follow-Up

People have limited time to prepare for meetings. Yet paradoxically, the lack of preparation can lead to unproductive meetings that take up a lot of time. The All-in-One Agenda is a tool that expedites meeting preparation and can also be used during meetings to compensate for lack of preparation.

ALL-IN-ONE AGENDA

The All-in-One Agenda format[4] on pages 152 and 153 is designed to streamline meeting preparation, execution, and design. The agenda has a front and back (or two separate pages). The front page has the meeting title, location, date, meeting purpose, meeting results, and the timed agenda. These elements are completed before the meeting.

A number of areas are left blank for the meeting participants to use during the meeting. These include columns for the participants to track the progress made in accomplishing the individual meeting results listed on the agenda.

A Notes column lets participants make notes during each time segment. At the bottom of the first page, an area is set aside to document the action commitments made during the meeting.

On the second (or back) page of this template, you'll see room for notes and an abbreviated composition analysis for the participant's use. Additional items may be included, such as norms the group uses to regulate meeting behavior or tools the group might use, such as reminders about MBTI communication preferences. Of course, it may be necessary to go to multiple pages for a long or complex meeting.

CHECKLISTS: USING DATA TO ACHIEVE RESULTS

A companion tool for the All-in-One Agenda is a series of checklists that enable you to collect data about the three stages necessary for meeting effectiveness: preparation, meeting implementation, and meeting follow-up. The design of the checklists ensures that the essential tasks for each stage are accomplished and that information can be gathered and analyzed to assess effectiveness and improve effectiveness over time.

The convener, facilitator, co-facilitator, and members of the co-design team can use the checklists to guide the meeting planning, execution, and follow-up.

A fourth checklist can be used by participants. The participant checklist is also organized into the three stages of getting ready, moving to action and producing results, and collecting information that can illuminate what the participant is doing to contribute to achieving results. This checklist enables participants to see how preparation for and participation in meetings contribute to action after meetings that lead to results.

The checklist can be used by anyone participating in meetings as a personal guide to his/her own effectiveness, or it can be used by a group of participants in conjunction with those convening and facilitating meetings to create a robust data set for ongoing quality improvement and learning.

ALL-IN-ONE AGENDA

Come with meeting results in mind and leave with action commitments in hand

Meeting Title	
Date and Time	
Location	

MEETING PURPOSE

MEETING RESULTS	ACCOMPLISHED	SOME PROGRESS	NOT ADDRESSED	NEXT STEPS
Ready to work together				
Action commitments made				

AGENDA

TIME	TASK/RESULT	NOTES: INSIGHTS, DECISIONS, NEXT STEPS
	Task: Welcome, purpose, check-in Result: Ready to work together	
	Task: Result:	
	Task: Result:	
	Task: Check-out Result: Action commitments made	
	Adjourn	

LEAVE WITH ACTION COMMITMENTS

Who needs to take action?	What actions will move the group forward?	When will the process start and end?	Why is this action a priority?

Meeting Title	
Date and Time	
Location	

NOTES

COMPOSITION ANALYSIS

Name	Organization	Role	Contribution/ Connection

CONVENER/FACILITATOR CHECKLISTS

The items on this checklist may be helpful in preparing for your meeting. The checklist data can be charted to create a trend line of how well meetings are going and what happens after meetings, to see if people are moving to action and achieving results. This information is used to inform future meeting design, execution, and facilitation.

1. Before the Meeting: Preparing	
Connected	
___# participants	Composition Analysis ___% participants with connection to each other ___% participants with connection to the result
Actionable	
___# results	Meeting Results ___% results clear enough to tell whether accomplished or not ___% results within B/ART of participants
Engaging	
___# meeting agenda topics	Meeting Agenda Topic Design ___% agenda topics starting with EQs and LFs ___% agenda topics with small group work or paired conversation
Informed	
___# days before meeting pre-work sent	Ready to Work ___% agenda topics designed to use pre-work ___% agenda topics used in the meeting distributed as pre-work
2. During the Meeting: Making Progress	
Results Focused	
___# results accomplished	Next Steps ___% participants who made action commitments ___% time spent on relationship building, problem solving, decision making, accountability, and action commitments
Relationship Oriented	
___# invitees present at meeting	Bonds Strengthened ___% participants referencing others in action commitments ___% absent participants to be contacted after the meeting
3. After the Meeting: Executing	
Getting It Done	
___# action commitments accomplished	Action Taken ___% participants reported on action commitment progress ___% participants who took action between meetings
Making a Difference	
___# performance measures trending in right direction	Aligned Action ___% participants using how much, how well performance measures to track effect of action commitments ___% participants using what-difference-did-we-make performance measures to align action commitments

PARTICIPANT CHECKLIST

As meeting participant, a checklist similar to the Convener/Facilitator Checklist might be helpful.

Preparing (before the meeting)	
Connected	
___# meeting results I am interested in	
Engaged	
___# ideas of what I can contribute to achieving result	
Prepared	
___% of pre-work I completed before the meeting	
Prioritized	
___# minutes I arrived before the start of the meeting	
Moving to Action (during the meeting)	
Results Focused	
___% time I was actively engaged	Next Steps ____# action commitments made ____# times provided candid feedback or did honest self-assessment
Relationship Oriented	
___% meeting participants I got to know better	Bonds Strengthened ____% action commitments connected to other participants ____# absent participants I will contact after the meeting
Producing Results (after the meeting)	
Getting It Done	
___% my action commitments accomplished	Action Taken ___% action commitments put on calendar ___% action on commitments worked on with others
Making a Difference	
____% performance measures trending in right direction	Aligned Action ____% action commitments where I am using how much, how well performance measures to track effect ____% action commitments where I am using what-difference-did-we-make performance measures to work with others

Often as a participant you are attending meetings that are not well planned or executed. On the next page are tips for using the 3Rs framework in meetings in the participant role.

TIPS: USING THE 3Rs IN A MEETING

If you are attending a meeting as a participant, you can do several things before and during the meeting to make it a 3R experience.

- If the convener or facilitator has not distributed a version of the All-in-One Agenda as shown in this chapter, you can make and bring your own.
- Prepare for the meeting as if you were the convener and envision meeting results to which you can contribute.
- During the meeting, use the Participant Practice Guide below to inform your participation.

PARTICIPANT PRACTICE GUIDE 4.2:
USE THE 3Rs IN THE MEETING TO ACHIEVE RESULTS

As a participant, there are many opportunities to greatly influence the productivity of meetings. This Participant Practice Guide provides examples of how to use the 3R framework to make meetings more productive.

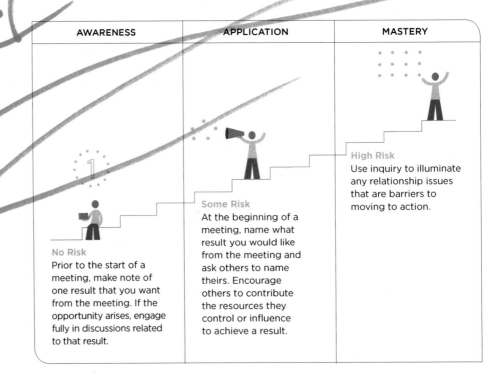

AWARENESS	APPLICATION	MASTERY
No Risk Prior to the start of a meeting, make note of one result that you want from the meeting. If the opportunity arises, engage fully in discussions related to that result.	**Some Risk** At the beginning of a meeting, name what result you would like from the meeting and ask others to name theirs. Encourage others to contribute the resources they control or influence to achieve a result.	**High Risk** Use inquiry to illuminate any relationship issues that are barriers to moving to action.

NOTES:

[1] MBTI Awareness at Person-Role-System Level (www.rbl-apps.com)

[2] *Creating the Container to Achieve Results* by Patton Stephens (2015) provides additional details and useful information for creating the ideal setting for RBF meetings.

[3] Include breaks and meals as appropriate. In general, breaks every 1 1/2–2 hours are helpful to the participants.

[4] Celia Cockfield and Bill Buckner of the Annie E. Casey Foundation supported the design and testing of the All-in-One Agenda and Checklists.

PATHWAY TO ADVANCED SKILLS

In this chapter, you'll find ways to practice the skills and competencies you have learned in this book and prepare to move to the advanced RBF skills in Book Two. Techniques include mnemonic devices for daily practice, methods for sustained deliberate practice and a blueprint for creating your individual development plan.

» **Advanced skills:** the skill set used to facilitate improvement of population results

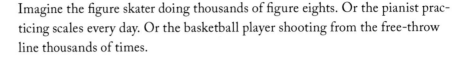

Imagine the figure skater doing thousands of figure eights. Or the pianist practicing scales every day. Or the basketball player shooting from the free-throw line thousands of times.

Mastery is attained when the use of the skill seems effortless to others, but the path to mastery is through dedicated skill practice. Consider the exchange between the interviewer and water colorist Gary Bukovnik (see left margin).[1]

In these examples, practice creates mastery. In this same way, disciplined practicing will create mastery of the foundation skills (technique) and build the platform for mastery of advanced skills. At this point in your RBF skill development, you have had the opportunity to develop four foundation competencies:

1. Hold Roles
2. Hold Conversations
3. Hold Groups
4. Hold 3R Meetings

The path to mastery in these skills is practice — practice of sufficient quantity and quality to achieve mastery of these skills and to prepare you to master the advanced skills. But, as the authors in *Practice Perfect*[2] know, practicing isn't enough.

> [H]ow you practice matters as much if not more than how much you practice. Practicing the wrong way can solidify poor performance. Practicing the right way involves breaking through assumptions, modeling excellent practice, using feedback, creating a culture of practice, making new skills stick.

The invitation to you is to find your own methods of daily, deliberate practice and to incorporate those practice methods into a development plan focused on the skills that are important to you.

DAILY PRACTICE

One's daily work and experience provide the best opportunity for the repetitive, constant practice needed for mastery. The challenge is to change your habitual way of doing things and to incorporate a new practice that contributes to mastering the skill.

Many practitioners use mnemonics — short memorable phrases — to help them remember and apply what they know in their daily work. The following table offers examples of daily and deliberate practice that may inform the choices you make for your own development. The table provides examples of mnemonics and how practitioners have used them to integrate the skills into their daily practice:

MNEMONIC	COMPETENCY	APPLICATION
You, not we	**HOLD ROLES**	When facilitating, people refer to the group as we, including themselves in the group. When holding neutral, the facilitator is not part of the group and, therefore, would always refer to the group as you. Instead of saying: We will now brainstorm, the facilitator would say, This is an opportunity for you to brainstorm as a group. Changing this speech habit is difficult. One facilitator made a bracelet with the message UNOTWE to remind herself to use the language of holding neutral.
Breathing and body breaks	**HOLD CONVERSATIONS**	Group members and facilitators can get caught up in conversations and/or disengaged from conversations, which effectively shuts down the listening. Using this mnemonic helps people practice mindfulness — a practice that encourages people to become more aware in the moment of their thoughts, feelings, bodily sensations, and environment. To use mindfulness during a meeting, the facilitator pauses the conversation. She encourages participants to notice the tension in their bodies, slow down, and focus on their breathing for a count of 10, or take a brief moment to release tension in their shoulders or bodies. The practice is enhanced by setting the context for the breathing break as a useful technique for increasing the capacity of the group to listen to each other. A participant or a facilitator can use this technique unobtrusively and quietly to focus and sustain appreciative openness during conversations.
Tables and Tents	**HOLD GROUPS**	A practice that engages people is to ask smaller groups of people sitting together in tables of six to seven to have a conversation and share their table perspective with the larger group. The smaller group is asked to turn their name tents to a vertical position to indicate when they are ready to share their work or go on to the next conversation. Practitioners use this mnemonic to remind themselves to pay attention to when the tents are turned vertically and to stay conscious of the group's pace and engagement level. As groups complete their work and turn their tents, the facilitator announces to the rest: "Three tables have turned their tents up," keeping the group aware of pace, as well.
Hands, head, heart	**HOLD 3R MEETINGS**	In reaching consensus, people benefit from having the opportunity to process information both intellectually and emotionally. Hands, head, heart is a mnemonic to remind practitioners to give people the time to first have something in their hands that they can read, then the opportunity to think about what they have read, and then to engage with others to explore reactions. In using this mnemonic, facilitators, participants, or meeting conveners can slow down and make sure everyone has a copy of the relevant material, has the time to read it, and can make notes to themselves about what they think and feel. Then they are ready to respond to EQs that elicit thoughts and feelings evoked by the information.

You can use these mnemonics or develop your own. Use the reflective practice questions to develop ways to integrate skills into your daily practice.

- What is a skill you want to remember to use?
- What will help you to remember — A phrase? A physical object? An image?

DELIBERATE PRACTICE

In traveling the practice path to mastery, two fundamental concepts accelerate skill development. One is the amount of practice (how much) and the other is the quality of the practice (how well). Ericsson, in studying the achievement of mastery in a number of fields, developed the concept of deliberate practice, a type of practice that differed from mere experience and mindless drill.[3] Ericsson discovered that the practice of people who achieved mastery in many fields was characterized by prolonged effortful activities designed to optimize performance.[4]

Examples of what deliberate practice looks like can be found in fields as diverse as music, chess, mathematics, and sports. This is what deliberate practice looks like for a golfer:

> *Hitting an eight-iron 300 times with a goal of leaving the ball within 20 feet of the pin 80 percent of the time, continually observing results and making appropriate adjustments, and doing that for hours every day — that's deliberate practice.*[5]

The following guidance applies the principles of deliberate practice to RBF and suggests RBF tools and resources to aid you in moving to mastery.

1. **Use skill assessments to identify specific skills that need development, and use practice methods to strengthen those skills.**

TOOL: The RBF Competency Assessments in the appendices point to areas of needed development and offer benchmarks of progress.

TOOL: The Individual Development Plan for each competency (also in the appendices) captures the specifics of what you will do and links to practice methods for skill improvement.

2. **Use feedback to track the impact of your skills development and enhance practice methods.**

TOOL: The Situation, Behavior, Impact form, found in the Practice: Developing RBF Skills chapter, provides data to track and inform skill development.

TOOL: The All-in-One 3R Agenda, found in Competency 4, provides a way to document meeting results accomplished. Tracked over time, use of the agenda provides information on how the use of skills affects achieving meeting results and engaging participants.

TOOL: The check-ins create feedback by establishing or affirming meeting results at the beginning, and the check-outs assess progress toward meeting results at the end.

3. **Take risks to stretch beyond the skills you know well. To develop mastery in those you are working on, in particular, be willing to try new skills and learn from failure and success.**

TOOL: The Participant Practice Guides found in each competency section offer suggestions for daily practice and ways to stretch practice to higher skill levels.

TOOL: A Qualified RBF Coach[6] can help you see the skills and get direction and feedback.

TOOL: Forming a learning partner relationship with a fellow practitioner committed to skill mastery can help you stay on track.

Take the time now to reassess your skill level for each foundation competency using the following assessment matrix.

COMPETENCY ASSESSMENT OF RBF SKILLS

RBF COMPETENCIES AND SKILLS	SKILL LEVEL/CONTINUUM		
	AWARENESS	APPLICATION	MASTERY
HOLD ROLES: *Be aware of and make choices about roles that contribute to achieving results.*			
Use B/ART to define and differentiate roles as they relate to meeting results			
Use B/ART to understand group dynamics and achieve meeting results			
Hold neutral facilitator role			
Give the work back to the group			
HOLD CONVERSATIONS: *Listen with openness, curiosity, and attentiveness to frame dialogues that achieve meeting results.*			
Demonstrate appreciative openness			
Use Context Statements, Effective Questions, and Listen Fors			
HOLD GROUPS: *Support groups in having focused conversations that move to results.*			
Use flip chart to display the group's work			
Sequence			
Summarize			
Synthesize			
Check in and check out			
HOLD 3R MEETINGS: *Use the 3R framework to design and facilitate meetings that move groups from talk to action.*			
Use the 3Rs to design the meeting			
Use the 3Rs in the meeting to achieve results			

INDIVIDUAL DEVELOPMENT PLAN

As you integrate and master the skills, you will notice the following associated benefits:

> » an increased ability to collaborate with others and accelerate progress toward results;

> » a heightened awareness of your strengths and how to deploy them to achieve results; and

> » an enhanced ability to notice the impact of your skills and to learn from experience.

As you realize these benefits, you will find that you can more predictably create and contribute to coherent conversations that address and resolve issues and that move you and others to accountable, aligned action. However, you may also find that there are times when moving from talk to action is beyond your current skill set.

Based on your competency assessment, you now have an opportunity to create an individual development plan for yourself that addresses the specific areas where you are interested in building skill.

PRACTICE: ANALYZING SKILL DEVELOPMENT OPPORTUNITIES

1. Look at your competency assessment. Are there any skills in the Hold Roles or Hold Conversations competencies where you are not at least at the application level? If so, focus on those skills for your individual development plan (IDP). Building skills in these competencies is a prerequisite for mastery of all the other skills.

2. Consider your daily work. Are there challenges that need to be addressed that present you with opportunities to develop skills in an intentional way? Consider the following examples of daily opportunities:

   • One-on-one phone calls with colleagues or family members to practice appreciative openness and to be more fully present and engaged at every moment of the call.

   • Conference calls with colleagues to practice doing a composition analysis of the B/ART of each participant, using EQs and LFs to elicit commitments to action within their B/ART.

   • Discussion with a neighbor about a contentious topic to practice Acknowledge, Rephrase, Explore (ARE) and to understand your neighbor's point of view.

   • A 3R agenda for a team meeting you are leading to ensure that the time is used efficiently and effectively.

   • Charting key points and decisions for a staff meeting that you are attending.

   • Using a CS and EQ in an email or a memo to elicit feedback from the recipient.

   • Using MBTI insights in a conversation with a family member or colleague to inform how you communicate.

3. Use the format of the IDP to identify the skill(s) to develop, what specifically you will do to build the skill, how and where you will practice daily, and what the desired impact is of using the skill. The key to skills development is to find ways to practice them daily in multiple settings to achieve a higher skill level. If you wait to practice skills until you most need them — for example, in a high-stakes, large public meeting — you will not have had enough repetition and time on task to develop the skills. Unless your full-time role is to be a facilitator (and even then, most people do not facilitate every day), you must find ways to practice the skills in your daily work.

4. Pay attention to the quality of your practice and the impact of your use of skills. The Convener and Participant Checklists found in Competency 4 provide useful information for tracking the impact of your skills. Use information and observation to note the impact of your practice when you review and revise your IDP. Use the IDP to reinforce habits that help you incorporate the principles of deliberative practice into what you do daily.

The example IDP below shows how to practice RBF skills. As the example highlights, an important part of deliberate practice is observing the impact of your practice and using those observations to improve your skill level. The IDP format, by connecting daily, skill-focused effort with observation of impact, is designed to accelerate your progress and ensure that you and those around you derive benefit from your application of skill.

EXAMPLE INDIVIDUAL DEVELOPMENT PLAN

Skill/Present Level	What will I practice to build skill?	Where and how will I practice daily?	What is the desired impact of improving the skill?
Charting — my handwriting is not legible Level: Awareness	The formation and spacing of letters	Use a flip chart in my office for key decisions from conversations with subordinates; pay attention to using the flat edge of the marker and making the letters 2 1/2 inches high.	My subordinates will be able to easily read the decisions, and we will refer to them to ensure execution. I will note the impact of my charting and request an SBI from my subordinates about the usefulness.

PRACTICE: IMPLEMENTING THE IDP

Review your IDP and reflect on the following questions to increase the likelihood that you will move forward and implement your plan:

• What strengths will support me in following through on this plan?

• Who can support and challenge me to be accountable for my own development?

• How can I notice the benefits of my practice and sustain my motivation to practice?

• What do I need to practice to hold neutral as a facilitator?

MOVING TO BOOK TWO (ADVANCED SKILLS)

As you practice the foundation skills, you may find yourself in situations that require more advanced competencies. For example, you may be looking for skills to help groups stuck in conflict, paralyzed by the inability to make collective decisions, or unable to hold themselves accountable for implementation. *Results Based Facilitation: Book Two — Advanced Skills* builds on the foundation skills with two additional competencies.

The Hold Mental Models competency is composed of seven skills that enable groups to use new ways of thinking.

HOLD MENTAL MODELS: *Use a repertoire of perspectives that contribute to achieving meeting results.*
Use proposal-based decision making to move from talk to action
Use conversations to develop convergence
Name and address barriers to convergence
Make and help others make action commitments
Be and help others be accountable for action commitments
Observe and respond to group dynamics
Assess and address conflict

The Hold Action and Results competency focuses on how RBF skills and methods are used. The competency includes the ability to design, participate in, and/or facilitate conversations and meeting designs that are effective in accomplishing the following:

> adopting a common result and ways to measure progress toward that result;

> committing to and being accountable for aligned actions that implement collaborative strategies; and

> developing the capacity to address differences across the boundaries of sector, gender, race, ethnicity, and world view to build the sustainable relationships necessary to persist in action long enough and well enough to make a measurable difference.

HOLD ACTION AND RESULTS: *Make a difference in programs and community populations.*
Be accountable in role for contributions to results
Use RBF skills to work collaboratively to accelerate progress toward results

You can find books, other materials, and tools on *www.rbl-apps.com*. Many of the agendas, templates, and worksheets from the examples, exercises, and tips have been posted on the website.

In addition, support for the practice and development of the foundation and advanced skills can be found through the Results Based Facilitation Network. The mission of the network is to support the application and integration of results based facilitation skills. You can connect to this network at *www.rbfnetwork.com*.

NOTES:

1. Interview of Gary Bukovnik by Claire Henry. November 2004.
2. Lemov, Woolway, and Yezzi. *Practice Perfect: 42 Rules for Getting Better at Getting Better.* Jossey-Bass. 2012.
3. Ericsson, Roring, and Nandagopal. Giftedness and evidence for reproducibly superior performance. *High Ability Studies,* Vol. 18, No. 1. June 2001.
4. Ericsson, Krampe, and Tesch-Römer. (1993). The role of deliberate practice in the acquisition of expert performance. *Psychological Review,* Vol. 100, No. 3, 363-406. 1993.
5. Colven. What it takes to be great. *Fortune Magazine.* October 19, 2006.
6. Find qualified RBF coaches on the rbfnetwork.com website.

COMPETENCY ASSESSMENTS AND IDPS

An IDP is included after each of the competency self-assessments to support you in designing skill-focused practice for each skill.

Hold Roles: Be aware of and make choices about roles that contribute to achieving results.

SKILL 1.1: USE B/ART TO DEFINE AND DIFFERENTIATE ROLES

AWARENESS	APPLICATION	MASTERY
Understands the concept of B/ART	Consciously establishes role in groups	Uses awareness of B/ART to contribute to meeting results and move from talk to action
• *Do I understand the Person-Role-System framework?*	• *Do I comfortably name my role in meetings?*	• *Do I consciously make choices to hold my stated role during a meeting?*
• *Do I know and can I name my own B/ART in my daily work and in meetings?*	• *Do I understand the differences in my various roles?*	• *Do I use my understanding of B/ART to align my actions with others to achieve results?*

SKILL 1.2: USE B/ART TO UNDERSTAND GROUP DYNAMICS AND ACHIEVE MEETING RESULTS

AWARENESS	APPLICATION	MASTERY
Applies the concept of B/ART to understand group dynamics	Applies B/ART insights to assist groups in identifying and achieving meeting results	Accurately identifies B/ART issues and brings these issues to the group's awareness
• *Do I use the Person-Role-System framework to assess the B/ART of meeting participants and consider how their B/ART will affect their participation?*	• *Do I clarify or help the group clarify the alignment of meeting results with the B/ART of the participants?*	• *Do I see how B/ART is affecting the group's work and then use labeling, inquiry, or hypotheses to illuminate the issues for the group?*
	• *Do I model awareness of B/ART in meetings?*	• *Do I map who in the group holds the B/ART to address issues, make decisions, and move to action?*

SKILL 1.3: HOLD NEUTRAL FACILITATOR ROLE

AWARENESS	APPLICATION	MASTERY
Knows the role of neutral facilitator and is aware of what it takes not to seek one's own personal agenda • *Do I employ specific practices to maintain the neutral facilitator role and not use the authority of the facilitator to pursue my own agenda?*	Holds the neutral role most of the time • *Do I refrain from using my expertise or authority to influence group decisions?* • *Do I recognize when I am not holding the neutral facilitator role?*	Consistently holds the neutral role • *Do I have a repertoire of practices to acknowledge lapses and return to neutral?*

SKILL 1.4: GIVE THE WORK BACK TO THE GROUP

AWARENESS	APPLICATION	MASTERY
Understands the role of the facilitator in giving the work back to the group • *Do I refer questions about the work back to the group?* • *Do I patiently hold the neutral facilitator role while the group takes time to find its own solutions and make its own decisions?*	Applies a repertoire of methods to give the work back to the group • *Do I recognize pivotal moments when to give the work back to the group?* • *Do I go to the balcony to invite group awareness and insights for forward movement?*	Consistently gives the work back to the group • *Do I use observation, inquiry, and reflective practice to invite the group to move forward?* • *Do I use humor, physical activity, intuition, spiritual awareness, and analytical insights to illuminate the group's capacity to do its hardest work?*

IDP: HOLD ROLES

SKILL/ PRESENT LEVEL	WHAT WILL I PRACTICE TO BUILD SKILL?	WHERE AND HOW WILL I PRACTICE DAILY?	WHAT IS THE DESIRED IMPACT OF IMPROVING THE SKILL?

Hold Conversations: Listen with openness, curiosity, and attentiveness to frame dialogues that achieve meeting results.

SKILL 2.1: DEMONSTRATE APPRECIATIVE OPENNESS

AWARENESS	APPLICATION	MASTERY
Understands the primacy of listening as a skill; is aware of and monitors own listening behavior	Attends to participants to ensure all ideas and voices are heard	Consistently demonstrates interest in conversations of others throughout the meeting
• *Am I genuinely curious about the conversation and what is being said?* • *Am I aware of when I am consciously listening and when I am not?* • *Do I make conscious choices about when to speak and when to listen?*	• *Am I aware of filters that may influence what is heard and not heard for myself and others?* • *Do I use strategies to remain open, appreciative, and in the moment?* • *Do I use nonverbal cues of attentiveness and interest?* • *Do I ask Effective Questions (EQs) to gain insight into assumptions, facts, and points of view and verify understanding of what was said?*	• *Do I keep my own interests and interpretations in check (be neutral) when I am listening?* • *Do I use a variety of strategies to engage the speaker (e.g., silence, non-verbal, EQs)?* • *Do I quickly notice lack of listening, acknowledge the lack, and self-correct?* • *Do I maintain focused listening for the duration of a meeting?*
→	→	→

SKILL 2.2: USE CONTEXT STATEMENTS, EFFECTIVE QUESTIONS, AND LISTEN FORS

AWARENESS	APPLICATION	MASTERY
Understands and uses CS, EQs, LFs as a core technique for facilitating	Frames the work (purpose, focus, boundary) with a CS, EQ, and LF in the moment	Regularly uses CS, EQs, and LFs to accelerate a group's ability to achieve meeting results
• *Do I set a context to focus a conversation on a meeting result?* • *Do I prepare EQs in advance to engage people, focus discussion, and move conversations forward toward meeting results?* • *Do I integrate a CS with an EQ and link it to an LF?*	• *Do I use EQs (open ended, inquisitive) to engage people, focus conversations, and move conversations forward toward meeting results?* • *Do I listen for responses and incorporate them into the group's work by setting another CS and linked EQ?*	• *Do I use CS, EQs, LFs to understand the group's experience of pace and adjust the pace to sustain maximum engagement?* • *Do I use awareness of differential impact (as informed by MBTI and B/ART) in CS, EQs, LFs?* • *Do I flexibly modify or change a CS, EQs, LFs in the moment based on my reading of the group?*
→	→	→

IDP: HOLD CONVERSATIONS

SKILL/ PRESENT LEVEL	WHAT WILL I PRACTICE TO BUILD SKILL?	WHERE AND HOW WILL I PRACTICE DAILY?	WHAT IS THE DESIRED IMPACT OF IMPROVING THE SKILL?

Hold Groups: Support groups in having focused conversations that move to results.

SKILL 3.1: USE FLIP CHART TO DISPLAY THE GROUP'S WORK

AWARENESS	APPLICATION	MASTERY
Displays group's work accurately	Displays group's work to focus on meeting results	Displays group's work to accelerate progress toward achieving meeting results
• *Do people read what is captured? Is it accurate?* • *Do I use the Context Statement, Effective Questions and Listen Fors to inform what is captured?* • *Does the speaker recognize what was said in what I captured?* • *Do I easily capture parallel conversations and accurately record decisions?*	• *Do my charts serve as a tool to recap work for summary?* • *Do I use techniques (color, underlining, symbols, spacing, lines) to highlight, track, and distinguish conversations?* • *Do people who were not in the conversation know its content from what is charted?* • *Do group members look at and refer to my charts?*	• *Do my charts support the building of proposals and making decisions?* • *Does my charting support synthesis and movement toward meeting results?* • *Do my charts support accountability for action during and after the meeting?*

SKILL 3.2: SEQUENCE

AWARENESS	APPLICATION	MASTERY
Understands and practices sequencing speakers	Understands and practices sequencing topics or ideas	Understands and practices sequencing the work of meetings and meeting results
• *Do I establish who speaks when in a way that is clear to the group and enables participants to relax and listen?*	• *Do I recognize different topics or conversations, label them, and invite the group to choose which conversation to have when?*	• *Do I recognize opportunities for proposals, decisions, and commitments to action and invite the group to sequence them during the meeting to accomplish meeting results?*

SKILL 3.3: SUMMARIZE

AWARENESS	APPLICATION	MASTERY
Remembers and can list ideas from short conversations • *Do I have a way to practice hearing, accurately remembering, and restating a list of ideas that emerges from a conversation?*	Remembers and can list categories of topics from medium to long conversations • *Do I concisely and accurately describe the content of conversations?* • *Do my summaries move a group forward toward the meeting results?*	Remembers and can briefly list process description or meeting results from a whole meeting • *Do I mentally review and then concisely state what has occurred in the meeting and the results achieved?*
→	→	→

SKILL 3.4: SYNTHESIZE

AWARENESS	APPLICATION	MASTERY
Briefly states the meaning of short conversations • *Do I listen for the central meaning of the conversation and state that concisely?* • *Do I use basic methods of synthesis (comparison, themes, part/whole connections) in listening for and concisely stating where the group is in their work?*	Integrates and briefly states the meaning of a number of conversations or longer conversations • *Does the group affirm my synthesis and use it to move forward to meeting results?* • *Do I use images and symbolism to help the group own the results of a whole meeting?*	Integrates and briefly states the meaning for a whole meeting • *Does my synthesis accelerate the group's work?* • *Does the group use my synthesis to move to action?*
→	→	→

SKILL 3.5: CHECK IN AND CHECK OUT

AWARENESS	APPLICATION	MASTERY
Understands and uses check-in and check-out	Connects group members to each other and the meeting results	Reads group to inform check-in and check-out
• *Does my check-in establish a foundation for the group to own the achievement of meeting results?* • *Do my check-outs assess meeting results and move people to action?*	• *Do I consider the relationships of the people to each other and the work in framing the check-in and check-out?* • *Do my check-ins and check-outs illuminate B/ART and make it more likely that members will contribute their resources to the meeting results?* • *Do my check-outs address whether meeting results were achieved and elicit how group members felt about the meeting experience?*	• *Do I use the technique of checking in and out flexibly during a series of conversations, or do I facilitate transitions from one meeting result to another?* • *Do I use check-in or check-out to explore hypotheses about group dynamics or make the group aware of group dynamics?* • *Do my check-ins and check-outs at the beginning and end of meetings and the beginning and end of conversations move a group to action?*

SKILL/ PRESENT LEVEL	WHAT WILL I PRACTICE TO BUILD SKILL?	WHERE AND HOW WILL I PRACTICE DAILY?	WHAT IS THE DESIRED IMPACT OF IMPROVING THE SKILL?

Hold 3R Meetings: Use the 3R framework to design and facilitate meetings that move groups from talk to action.

AWARENESS	APPLICATION	MASTERY
Understands the interrelationship and use of the 3Rs as they relate to the design of a meeting agenda • *Do I clearly articulate the results for meetings (specific, observable, measurable)?* • *Do the proposed meeting results contribute to a program or organizational result?*	Uses EQs and LFs to elicit what the group wants to accomplish, who is and needs to be involved, and what people have and can bring to achieve the desired results • *Do I use B/ART in analyzing the composition of groups to explore who might be invited to contribute to meeting results?* • *Do I assess if those invited can accomplish the meeting results with their relationships and resources?*	Designs the meeting agenda and environment for the group to own its work by applying the 3Rs • *Do I align meeting preparation and design with the desired results?* • *Do I ensure that the required resources are accessible at the meeting?* • *Do I recognize and encourage people aligning their resources to achieve results?*
→	→	→

AWARENESS	APPLICATION	MASTERY
Understands the interrelationships and use of the 3Rs to help groups achieve results • *Do the meeting results align with the meeting purpose?* • *Do all meeting results add up to the purpose?*	Uses EQs and LFs with the group to elicit 3Rs during the meeting • *Do the CS, EQs, and LFs achieve the meeting result?*	Creates an environment for the group to own its work by applying the 3Rs. Captures decisions, commitments, etc., in a 3R framework • *Do I use the 3R framework to follow up on meetings to move from talk to action?* • *Do I capture decisions and commitments in terms of who will do what when, how, and with whom, and with what resources?*
→	→	→

SKILL/ PRESENT LEVEL	WHAT WILL I PRACTICE TO BUILD SKILL?	WHERE AND HOW WILL I PRACTICE DAILY?	WHAT IS THE DESIRED IMPACT OF IMPROVING THE SKILL?

Hold Mental Models: Use a repertoire of perspectives that contribute to achieving meeting results.

SKILL 5.1: USE PROPOSAL-BASED DECISION MAKING TO MOVE FROM TALK TO ACTION

AWARENESS	APPLICATION	MASTERY
Understands and uses proposal-based decision making	Synthesizes proposals and gives the work back to the group	Helps groups stay in the hard work of decision making
• *Do I make proposals and build on proposals?*	• *Do I concisely introduce the concept of PBDM?*	• *Do I attend to pace to support engagement?*
• *Do I set a context and ask an Effective Question to elicit proposals?*	• *Do I label proposals as options?*	• *Do I recognize when a group is not moving forward in decision making?*
• *Do I use the rule of thumb to scan levels of support?*		

SKILL 5.2: USE CONVERSATIONS TO DEVELOP CONVERGENCE

AWARENESS	APPLICATION	MASTERY
Frames conversations that move people toward convergence	Labels where the group is in the process of convergence and supports forward movement	Recognizes, labels, and synthesizes conversations to support the group's ability to make choices about what to do next
• *Does my synthesis of the group's work support movement toward convergence?*	• *Do I share observations about the group and invite others to share theirs?*	• *Can I support the group in making choices about the process of decision making?*
• *Do I set a context so the group can work with emotion-laden proposals?*	• *Can I use Effective Questions to move the group forward toward convergence?*	• *Do I regularly and quickly help groups choose the conversation that will move them forward?*

SKILL 5.3: NAME AND ADDRESS BARRIERS TO CONVERGENCE

AWARENESS	APPLICATION	MASTERY
Names divergent mental models	Uses mental models to develop solutions and make decisions	Uses a repertoire of mental models to address barriers
• Do I label my own mental models and listen for the mental models expressed by group members? • Can I use the ladder of inference or the 5 Fs (Feelings, Frames, Filters, Facts, Findings) to listen for other people's mental models?	• Do I apply the underlying concepts of interest-based negotiation to help the group develop solutions? • Do I use the MBTI communication preferences Z model to sequence discussions and move groups toward decisions?	• Do I readily identify and shift to another mental model to address barriers? • Can I use mental models that do not represent my own world view or values?
→	→	→

SKILL 5.4: MAKE AND HELP OTHERS MAKE ACTION COMMITMENTS

AWARENESS	APPLICATION	MASTERY
Understands the intent and form of effective action commitments	Helps groups commit to action	Helps groups align action commitments
• Do I set a context for making public action commitments? • Do I Listen For action commitments with a disciplined focus on who, what, and when? • Do I support the group in documenting action commitments for future reference?	• Do I help groups manage the change process associated with moving to action?	• Do I use MBTI awareness to support people making action commitments? • Can I use the High Action/ High Alignment framework?
→	→	→

SKILL 5.5: BE AND HELP OTHERS BE ACCOUNTABLE FOR ACTION COMMITMENTS

AWARENESS	APPLICATION	MASTERY
Understands and uses the Accountability Pathway	Helps groups hold accountability for action commitments	Strengthens the group's capacity to be accountable for action
• *Do I introduce the Account-ability Pathway as a method for people to keep commitments to action?* • *Am I comfortable and do I help others become comfortable holding genuine accountability conversations?*	• *Do I use EQs that make it easy for me and others to assess progress along the Accountability Pathway, move to owning action commitments, and make them happen?*	• *Do I label the emotional reactions of myself and others and use EQs to support the group in making and keeping commitments to action?* • *Do I use MBTI awareness to support groups in holding accountability for action?*
→	→	→

SKILL 5.6: OBSERVE AND RESPOND TO GROUP DYNAMICS

AWARENESS	APPLICATION	MASTERY
Maps who is saying what and what role he or she plays in the group	Observes, understands, and responds to patterns of behavior in groups	Helps groups move through difficult conversations
• *Do I notice and remember who is saying what when? Their affect? Their body language?* • *Do I see, label, and generate hypotheses about patterns in the group?* • *Do I consistently use the five-step process to create engagement?*	• *Do I respond to group behaviors in ways that give the work back to the group?* • *Do I observe pace and know when to slow down and when to speed up?*	• *Do I make in-the-moment observations about the group that enable it to move forward?* • *Do I invite group members to make observations about facts and feelings, generate hypotheses, and respond to what they observe in group?*
→	→	→

SKILL 5.7: ASSESS AND ADDRESS CONFLICT

AWARENESS	APPLICATION	MASTERY
Understands own and others' orientation toward conflict • *Do I understand my own and others' orientation toward conflict?* • *Do I accept that conflict is a fact of life that can be addressed and resolved?*	Introduces and applies the Circle of Conflict • *Can I apply the Circle of Conflict to identify sources of conflict?* • *Can I frame conversations that engage people in addressing the sources of conflict?*	Supports groups in addressing conflict and moving to action • *Do I use insights from MBTI awareness to design conversations to address conflict?* • *Do I integrate the application of the Circle of Conflict into PBDM?*

IDP: HOLD MENTAL MODELS

SKILL/ PRESENT LEVEL	WHAT WILL I PRACTICE TO BUILD SKILL?	WHERE AND HOW WILL I PRACTICE DAILY?	WHAT IS THE DESIRED IMPACT OF IMPROVING THE SKILL?

Hold Action and Results: Make a difference in programs and community populations.

SKILL 6.1: BE ACCOUNTABLE IN ROLE FOR CONTRIBUTIONS TO RESULTS

AWARENESS	APPLICATION	MASTERY
Makes contributions to a result	Is accountable for aligning contributions to a result	Addresses challenges and moves self and others into aligned action
• *Do I understand my potential contribution to the result in role and role-in-system?* • *Do I clarify and negotiate B/ART with others to contribute to the result?*	• *Do I use performance measures to assess and improve my and others' contributions to the result?* • *Do I mobilize my own and others' resources to make progress toward population-level results?*	• *Do I work to strengthen action and alignment of contributions over time?* • *Do I comfortably exercise heterarchical and hierarchical authority in aligning my contributions with others?*
→	→	→

SKILL 6.2: USE RBF SKILLS TO WORK COLLABORATIVELY TO ACCELERATE PROGRESS TOWARD RESULTS

AWARENESS	APPLICATION	MASTERY
Convenes, designs, documents, or facilitates meetings that put results in the center of the work	Convenes, designs, documents, or facilitates meetings where people are in high action and high alignment to make progress toward a result	Convenes, designs, documents, or facilitates meetings that sustain accountability for contributions at a scope and scale to accelerate progress toward a result
• *Do I work as a member of a team to design and execute meetings that move groups to make aligned action commitments to a population-level result?* • *Do I contribute to creating a container for aligned contributions to a result?*	• *Do I ensure that there are 3R meetings that move partners from talk to action that produces results?* • *Do I facilitate conversations that support aligned action?*	• *Do I persist in the face of uncertainty, or slow or no progress, to implement what works to make population-level change?* • *Do I take risks to challenge others to put results in the center of their work and contribute to population-level change?*
→	→	→

SKILL/ PRESENT LEVEL	WHAT WILL I PRACTICE TO BUILD SKILL?	WHERE AND HOW WILL I PRACTICE DAILY?	WHAT IS THE DESIRED IMPACT OF IMPROVING THE SKILL?

LIST OF PARTICIPANT PRACTICE GUIDES

Each of the skills can be used in the participant role. For easy reference, the following is a list of all Participant Practice Guides.

RBF COMPETENCIES AND SKILLS	Page
HOLD ROLES	
SKILL 1.1: Use B/ART to define and differentiate roles as they relate to meeting results	43
SKILL 1.2: Use B/ART to understand group dynamics and achieve meeting results	52
SKILL 1.3: Hold neutral facilitator role	62
SKILL 1.4: Give the work back to the group	69
HOLD CONVERSATIONS	
SKILL 2.1: Demonstrate appreciative openness	76
SKILL 2.2: Use Context Statements, Effective Questions, and Listen Fors	86
HOLD GROUPS	
SKILL 3.1: Use flip chart to display the group's work	94
SKILL 3.2: Sequence	101
SKILL 3.3: Summarize	106
SKILL 3.4: Synthesize	109
SKILL 3.5: Check in and check out	115
HOLD 3R MEETINGS	
SKILL 4.1: Use the 3Rs to design the meeting	125
SKILL 4.2: Use the 3Rs in the meeting to achieve results	140

LIST OF PRACTICES

The following is a list of the practices provided to support skill development. Not every skill in each competency has a practice.

LIST OF TIPS

In addition to practices, for many skills, tips are provided to support your application and use of the skills. As with the exercises, not all skills have tips.

APPENDIX C

TERM	DEFINITION
3Rs (Relationships, Resources, and Results)	Results Based Facilitation's underlying mental model for designing and executing meetings that produce results in programs, organizations, and communities.
5Fs	Feelings, Frames, Filters, Facts, Findings
Accountability Pathway	A mental model for helping people strengthen their ability to keep the commitments they make.
Acknowledge, Rephrase, and Explore (ARE)	A method to give the work back to the group through listening, providing empathetic responses, and asking open-ended questions.
Action Commitment Form	A template for recording and updating what people commit to do to improve a result. The format enables the assessment of both action and alignment and the tracking of completion.
Action Plan	A document to guide the implementation of and accountability for aligned actions to achieve a measurable improvement in a population-level results. The Action Plan contains the following elements: • population, result, indicator, and target for indicator improvement • factor analysis, strategies, performance measures for strategies and performance measure targets, and the action commitments with targets and timeline to implement the Action Plan
Adaptive Challenges	Heifetz term describing changes in behavior, beliefs, habits, or values.
Aligned Action	Complementary, supportive actions that people take together to make measurable progress toward a result.
Balanced Scorecard	A strategic planning and management system developed by Kaplan and Norton to align business activities to the vision and monitor organization performance against strategic goals.

TERM	DEFINITION
Best Alternative to a Negotiated Agreement (BATNA)	An articulation of how a party's interests might be met in the absence of reaching a negotiated agreement.
Boundaries of Authority, Role, and Task (B/ART)	The defined parameters that circumscribe and illuminate who is responsible (authority) for what activity (task) in what capacity in relationship to others and their activities (role).
Check-In	A process to facilitate connections to a person or people and a task. When checked in, people are ready to work together.
Check-Out	A process to facilitate the closing of a meeting or a conversation so people are committed to the next steps, ready to move on, and aware of the progress made toward their own results and the meeting results.
Circle of Conflict	A mental model developed by Christopher W. Moore to assess and address conflict by identifying categories of conflict.
Collaborative Work Cycle	A mental model of how to use meetings to move from talk to accountable, aligned action between meetings.
Composition Analysis	Information about the person, the person-in-role and his or her role in system. The information is used to clarify B/ART and inform hypotheses about group dynamics before, after, and during conversations and meetings.
Context Statement (CS)	A brief phrase or short sentence introducing a conversation that lets people know what the conversation is about.
Differential Impact	The varied reactions people have to a common experience.
Effective Questions (EQs)	Open-ended queries that convey curiosity and an invitation to share focused information relevant to the conversation.
Experiential Learning Cycle	Skill development grounded in a process that allows people to discover and learn what they need and want by reflecting on their own practice experiences, by seeing what their colleagues are doing, by using skills they want to learn, and by receiving feedback and coaching.
Friedman's Results Accountability Framework	Developed by Mark Friedman, a framework for defining and achieving conditions of well-being for programs and whole populations.

TERM	DEFINITION
Going to the Balcony	A mental stance described by Heifetz wherein a person gains perspective by imagining being on a balcony above the situation and looking down at the group dynamics to see one's own role and that of others.
Heterarchy	A system of organization characterized by overlap, multiplicity, mixed ascendancy, and/or divergent-but-coexistent patterns of relation.
High Action/High Alignment (HA/HA)	Action Commitments that are aligned to achieve greater impact for a common result. Groups are in high action and high alignment when each leader is making an impactful contribution that connects and strengthens the contributions of others to accelerate progress toward population results.
Hold 3R Meetings	The competency of using the 3R framework to design and facilitate meetings that move groups from talk to action.
Hold Action and Results	The competency to make a difference in programs and community populations.
Hold Conversations	The competency of listening with openness, curiosity, and attentiveness to frame dialogues that achieve meeting results.
Hold Groups	The competency of supporting groups in having focused conversations that move to results.
Hold Mental Models	The competency of using a repertoire of perspectives that contribute to achieving meeting results.
Hold Roles	The competency of being aware of and making choices about roles that contribute to achieving meeting results.
Individual Development Plan (IDP)	A template used to focus skill practice and competency development.
Interest-Based Negotiation (IBN)	Fisher and Ury's approach to negotiation where people listen to each other to find common ground and build win-win solutions.
Ladder of Inference	Argyris originated and Senge popularized this concept that illuminates connections and interactions between actions, beliefs, conclusions, assumptions, meaning, data, and experiences.
Leadership in Action Program (LAP)	A collaborative leadership development program where multisector leaders work together to make a measurable improvement in community well-being.
Listen Fors (LFs)	The ability to consciously focus on hearing clearly the specific content areas of a conversation.

TERM	DEFINITION
Mnemonic	A short phrase to help people remember and apply skills and practices in their daily work.
Myers-Briggs Type Indicator (MBTI)	A personality inventory of psychological types reflecting people's preferences for gaining energy, taking in information, making decisions, and organizing their lives.
Performance Partnership Summit (PPS)	One and a half day meetings implemented with RBF skills at which leaders create and commit to implement strategies to reduce smoking prevalence in their communities.
Person-Role-System (PRS)	A framework for understanding the interrelationship of a person's unique characteristics and qualities and the roles they play (consciously and unconsciously) in different systems.
Proposal-Based Decision Making (PBDM)	A mental model and a practice for collaborative decision making.
RBF Hypotheses	The three hypotheses that inform the theory and practice of Results Based Facilitation.
RBL-APPs	Results Based Leadership Applications — resources available on the *www.rbl-apps.com* website to implement RBF designs and support the development of results based leadership.
Result in the Center and Results in the Center Chart	An orientation when a population result is the center of one's work enabling an understanding of your relationship to the result, your contribution to the result, and your relationship to others who can or do contribute to the result. This orientation supports accountability for aligned action to make measurable improvement in population-level results. The Results in the Center chart is a template for mapping your and others' relationship to a result in the context of sector and role. This tool is useful in developing an awareness of the B/ART and leveraging contributions across sectors into aligned strategies.
Results Based Facilitation (RBF)	A competency-based approach to participating in and facilitating meetings that get results.
Results Based Leadership (RBL)	A competency-based approach to leadership that equips leaders to make contributions in role to a measurable improvement in programs or whole populations.
Robert's Rules of Order (model of advocacy and majority rule)	A method of formal decision making in which people debate each other and as advocates present arguments to convince others to support their idea. The idea is expressed as a motion, and a decision is made when debate is concluded and a majority of people vote in favor of a motion.

TERM	DEFINITION
Role	The function assumed or part played by a person in a particular situation.
Role Clarity	Conscious awareness and choice about the role in conversations, meetings, and groups with an understanding of the boundaries of authority, role, and task for that role in that time and place.
Scaffolding	An intentional sequencing of learning to support competency development.
Sequence	The skill of ordering people speaking in conversations, topics and/or meeting results.
Situation, Behavior, Impact (SBI)	A method of feedback on the impact of using RBF skills that describes the situation where the facilitation was experienced, the behavior of the facilitator, and the impact of the facilitation on the participant.
Stages of Change Model (Prochaska and DiClemente)	A mental model that illuminates six stages in the behavioral change process.
Summarize	The skill of listing the content of conversations or meetings.
Synthesize	The skill of bringing parts into a meaningful whole.
Theory of Aligned Contributions (TOAC)	People practicing a specific skill set can be in high alignment and high action toward a common result. Alignment means that people's actions are coordinated, leveraged, and sequenced to accelerate progress toward the measurable improvement in organizational and community conditions.
Wheel of Emotions (Plutchik)	A classification scheme developed by Plutchik to categorize and name a nuanced range of emotions.
Z model	Based on MBTI, a structured problem-solving approach that starts with facts, then develops options.

ABOUT THE AUTHOR

Jolie Bain Pillsbury, Ph.D., President of Sherbrooke Consulting, Inc., is the author of the two book set on Results Based Facilitation. Ms. Pillsbury is a cofounder of the Results Based Facilitation Network and the Results Based Leadership Consortium, and she is a founding co-director of the Results Based Leadership Collaborative at the University of Maryland School of Public Policy.

As a developer and practitioner of Results Based Leadership, she has authored the *Theory of Aligned Contributions,* which serves as the foundation for research and basis for continuous improvement in the effectiveness of results based leadership practice.

For more information visit, *www.sherbrookeconsulting.com, www.rbl-apps.com, www.rbfnetwork.com,* and *www.rblconsortium.com.*

Made in the USA
San Bernardino, CA
18 November 2017